MW01206190

Life SoFar

Arlo's Soul Talk

1

A Prophetic Journey: Unveiling the White Race's Origins

Chapter 1

What if the origins of the white race were intertwined with a biblical tale of divine punishment and migration? Uncover the fascinating journey of the ten tribes of Israel, exiled by the Assyrians for their transgressions, and their 2520-year odyssey that shaped the demographics of Europe and North America. From Scandinavia to the British Isles and Germany, explore the impact of these ancient tribes on modern populations. This narrative weaves together themes of divine planning, prophetic fulfillment, and the profound influence of historical migration on the establishment of the white race.

Venture further into the envisioned future city of God, a massive metropolis dominated by the white race, as we discuss who will find their names in Jesus Christ's book of life. Learn about the first resurrection's exemption from the second death and the grim fate awaiting those judged unfavorably. Reflect on the nature of God, His creation, and the importance of water, alongside a heartfelt personal story of miraculous recovery that underscores divine intervention and gratitude. The episode concludes with an emphasis on voluntary adherence to God's laws and a blessing that resonates deeply with faith and devotion.

Good evening. It's Arlo Johnson in Vernon, British Columbia. At about 8 o'clock pm on June the 8th, nice, warm day, very sunny, very warm, close to 80. It's a long day. Sunset is 9;10 or something like that. We're getting close to the longest day of the year, which would be June the 21st, and then we start going backwards again. It's a shame, you know, we just get the grass growing and some green grass around, and the next thing, you know, the days are getting shorter. But actually it seems to work out, I don't know, I wish it was a little later in the year, but that's the way it works.

Anyway, this is chapter one of the white race on this planet Period. There's been books written about the ten tribes of Israel and it's never been connected, you know, to the fact that God penalized them for breaking his law. I firmly believe that during the sixth day creation, all the races, all the different races, were created on the sixth day and , it appears to me that the white race maybe wasn't. Now, aboriginals have been around for a long time. You take, for instance, the Indians that ruled North America without being judgemental. They roamed from place to place following the buffalo ect. For thousands of years Now, I don't know how many thousands, but many thousands, occupying but not possessing the land.

Now the problem with that is when the English, the Scots, the Norwegians that were the first went to North America, they came from countries that had roads, buildings. They were making things, manufacturing things. They had ships and they had I don't know at that time if they would have had steam engines, but I think they had steam.They were factories making things, little factories, they were not big factories and they immigrated to this country they called North America. Now, when they got here, the Indians that roamed this great land hadn't built a stick of road, no infrastructure of any kind. They were hunters and fishers. That is how they lived. They lived off the land. They didn't possess the land. They occupied land and then moved and occupied other lands. They moved like the buffalo did. They moved with the grass. Now that means to me, when God has a plan, it's a great plan. It's so great it's beyond our understanding sometimes. But it appears to me that this was held in reserve for the children that he wanted to have on this planet, his future sons.

The ten tribes of Israel, if you look at the written record of it. they went off and they began to live like people do today. They ignored God completely. They had their own stuff and everything else, and God told them that for that reason they were,not to receive the Abrahamic blessings that God gave to Abraham to give to his sons and his prodigy after him. These were promises God made directly to these people, especially to Abraham, and he said he would be a blessing to the world and they would become like the sand of the sea. You have to remember the reason for all this is that God arranged a universe for you and I to exist in. It has to be just right. Everything has to be just right, weather conditions have to be just right, temperature has to be just right, temperature has to be just right, seasons to feed people and all the things that have to happen.

Now, when God determined that the ten tribes of Israel, the lost ten tribes of Israel, were going to be punished by a hold back in their, Abrahamic promises,They were going to be held back from that for 2520 years the Assyrians not Syrians, assyrians, god used the Assyrians to attack the entire ten tribes of Israel, all of them, took them all captive and took them out of Israel into Assyria and there were six million of them at that time. So we got to think about this Six million in the year whatever that year was . They were acting in God's timetable. Well, they didn't know that, Now, during that 2520 years, they traveled west, slowly, moving west through one area after another, until they got into the Caucasian mountains and I don't know, into Russia or northern China.They went all through that area and they were supposed to be a been, great horsemen, great horses and stuff like that. Now they kept going west, west.

God said in his writings and told his prophets he said I will sift them out of the nations. Now, remember that that's what he said. I will sift them out of the nations, obviously the nations of

1 Europe and Northern Europe, and all through Scandinavia, British Isles and Scotland, Ireland,
2 England. Now the promise here is that he was going to give them a promise after their penalty.
3 He's very fair in that. Now, during that time they multiplied. They must have multiplied and
4 multiplied until they become many millions.
5
6 Now there's records I suppose because people have written about this or and they claim that in
7 Germany alone there were approximately four million people immigrated out of Germany into
8 North America in I don't know, 1700s, 1800s, and not one of them was round-faced Assyrian type
9 German. They were all oval-shaped, norse-looking skulls, that is, round skulls stayed, the Nordic
10 skulls left. They all thought they were German. You know my take on this and what I'm proposing
11 to you is that that's where the white race came from. I don't know where else it could have come
12 from.
13
14 Europe was pretty well all a white race continent and the Isles of England, Ireland, Scotland, you
15 know, infiltrated or whatever you want to call it, by them developing and building and building in
16 Europe and then immigrating to North America, and this was the culmination of the Abrahamic
17 promise. That promise was riches, land, wealth, it said. I believe it said, like you know, the riches
18 of the deep, the riches of the womb, the riches of I forget. There are many things that are said
19 there, but they ended up with these white race people, and it didn't matter whether they were from
20 Ukraine or Germany or Norway or Sweden or England or Dutch, Holland or Ireland. They were
21 white race. Nobody thought about that at the time. There was nothing new about that. But now,
22 when you look at it, North America was held in abeyance for them all these years. Because that's
23 what happened. It's not maybe it was this or that. We're talking about history. That is what
24 happened. Canada became a white race nation. The United States was a white race nation.
25 Australia was a white race nation. South Africa wasn't totally white, but it was run by the white
26 people there because they took it over and I don't know what else. But North America, Australia,
27 and Europe were the best land in the world. It appears to me that all the riches come from the
28 land.
29
30 I was born and raised in Alberta, Canada, in the parkland area of central Alberta,where the black
31 dirt was three feet deep and you could grow crops like crazy there, and I've been away from there
32 now for about 60 years. I went back here a couple years ago, during the summertime, I think it was
33 in July and I drove down the same road that I drove on for 20 years, or 18, 20 years before I left
34 home home from where my dad's farm was, into town to Hay Lakes, which is six miles into town,
35 and go by all these farms. Every time I drive by the same field, same farm, the crop is like three or
36 four feet high, thick as hair on a dog, still producing Just as good or ever. You can't say that that
37 doesn't produce wealth. It does, it absolutely produces wealth. A grain of wheat dies and produces
38 a hundred, year after year, a hundred to one. All right, and now I think it's even more. I'm going to
39 get into something else here.

1

2 The white race seems to wake up Like when this 2,520 years were over. It was like the curse was
3 lifted and they started to build and do things. The Industrial Revolution kind of started then and
4 steam engines, ships, boats, railroads and our good friends in North America were still roaming
5 around. Now they want to collect their land. Well, they lived on it. It wasn't their land White race
6 has just been, you know, pretty generous. I know In this country, right here where I live, it's millions
7 of dollars after millions of dollars goes to the Indian Bands. They as a rule don't work. Government
8 supports them in many different ways.Some of them work.
9 Now, you know, there's a thing that ties in with this is that this has been going on now like what?
10 300, 500 years. Believe our cycle is just about over. You realize and this is in the Bible, there's no
11 getting around it that God and the Word decided, before there was a world, before the beginning of
12 the world, before the world, was that the Word who became Jesus Christ would suffer and die as a
13 result of the children and the people that God was going to create, and there was going to be
14 millions of them who couldn't keep his law, and the penalty for not keeping his law is death. Now, if
15 all his sons and all his children are breaking his law and he's a just God and he has to kill them all.
16 How is he going to get his sons for his kingdom? So Christ agreed, before there was anything, that
17 he would pay the price for God's children who would break his holy law. It's exactly what
18 happened.
19 Now we're at the point where this is all now winding down and it appears to me like it's going to
20 continue. The world was running , I would say you know, fairly decent and law abiding and
21 whatever else for a long time, until the last what? 20 years. And it's gone, just doomed. Right now
22 it's, it's scraping the bottom of the barrel and People say, well, this can't go on. Oh Well, it can go
23 on and God is going to most likely allow it to go on because people have broken all his laws and
24 when people break laws, there are penaltiesJesus said the last thing before he lifted off: don't be
25 Deceived. People just say, oh, he lifted and went ahead. How did that happen? What kind of
26 propulsion deal or magnetic deal is this? That you just go? But anyway, when he was lifting off, he
27 said don't be Deceived. That was the big thing and that is what's happening now.
28 As I sit here and talk to you today, we are being deceived wholesale, or worse. It wasn't that bad
29 ten years or 15 years ago. It's nice, just like it's being refined now. You people say it can't go on
30 like this. You know Well, it can go on like this and it will get worse. And God said there will be a
31 tribulation and there will be one-third to half of the people on this planet will die.
32
33 Well, I prefer to believe what he says, only what he says, not what anyone else says. And I would
34 suggest to you that if you believe what God has said through his prophets and whatever in the
35 Bible, and believe totally what Jesus Christ said in the three and a half years that he was here and
36 preached on earth and he got ready for the crucifixion to pay the penalty, and because the
37 problem is, the whole world is being deceived as I speak, there's no question about that the whole

1 world is blind to the fact that they're being deceived. They believe what they're told because they
2 don't know anything different. Why shouldn't they believe that they have no basis for not believing
3 it? There's no other news of some kind, very little anyway. So the business of being deceived is
4 great and it's going to hit this band of people on this planet, this generation, this little narrow band
5 of generational people now that are going to be hit hard, not the thousands of generations previous
6 all the way up, not them, not the people who have died it's not going to bother them but right now,
7 the people that are living right now I'd say 20 to 30 years old or something they're the ones that are
8 going to be hit hard, very hard. They're already Satan worshipers and Satan this and Satan that.
9 They have statues of Satan in some places in the States and they have satanic churches and
10 satanic groups and they're protected because, you know, we must not discriminate.(right)
11
12 Yeah, now, the book of Revelation is an eye-opener to anyone that wants to know what's going on,
13 what's going to happen and when, it doesn't give an exact date, but it says that that's what is going
14 to happen in the coming future. Sometimes, as it builds. I think that God has a plan, an actual plan
15 for everybody on the planet. He is that great he can be everywhere at once. His spirit can be
16 everywhere. His spirit obviously knows whatever is going on. His spirit never sleeps. He's given
17 directions in the book of Revelation about chapter 20, which you'd be well to read, and you can
18 find there the dimensions of the city that Jesus Christ talked about. He said I am going to prepare
19 a place for you that, where I am, you may be also.
20 Now Jesus laid out the criteria for being in his book of life, because the situation is this and Jesus
21 has explained it. God has explained it and said if you are not in Jesus Christ's book of life, when
22 the time comes for judgment, which is, you die. And then the judgment doesn't say when, but the
23 next thing that happens is the judgment. And then who is going to be in the judgment? To begin
24 with? Well, there's a good chance that it's going to be the people who are going to be in Christ's
25 book of life, and maybe that's what's going to be in the first resurrection. As he said, if you're in the
26 first resurrection, there's no second death for you. But if you are not, then he says, then is the
27 judgment, and the judgment penalty, is death, and you will be thrown into the lake of fire. Bang,
28 that's it, there's no getting around it. that's it, there's no getting around it.
29 People think, oh, god wouldn't do that. The thing is, God is not a man. He runs the universe in his
30 own way. Because he is the universe, everything is him, and that's hard to grasp, that he can
31 create a million stars and knows them all by name. He knows the hairs on everybody's head. Now,
32 don't you think it's a pretty good deal that God is who he is? You know what if he wasn't? What if
33 he wasn't ,a just and loving God, but also a fierce, fierce God. Fierce For those who break his
34 laws, all his things, if they purposely break it. He can be purposely viciously hard. He's, I believe,
35 now raised about a hundred billion people that in the world to come, they are all capable of being
36 his sons. That's what he talks about, only his sons.

Now, in the world to come, women will not be in the kingdom of God because there's no two sexes to argue and fight about things. There's no requirement for the womb. That's all done, and there's no need for jealousy and vanity, which are the two main problems that women have. Not that men don't have problems too, but the big problem is that what's ruined the whole universe is vanity and jealousy, first by Satan, jealous of God and vain in his beauty. That brought him down. Am I good-looking, am I beautiful, am I this? And then the next day, am I beautiful? You know. And yet, on the other hand, women are much better or stronger than men when it comes to suffering for children, patience and suffering, nurturing. You know Mothers have a place in God's eyes.

1 So if you believe what I've just said Now, the white race has been the shakers and the movers on
2 this planet. Basically, pretty well, not that the Chinese haven't done things In the last 50, 40, 50
3 years. It rose way up for most people. But if you read the book of Revelation, There it talks about
4 God's kingdom, 1500 miles square and 1500 miles high. That's his final city that will ever be in this
5 universe and it'll be populated by all his children who he's going to resurrect. You've got to be
6 pretty powerful to do these things. The building he's talking about is too big for this planet. Nobody
7 knew that or didn't talk about it. They didn't realize it until just lately. The four gates there's a gate
8 on each side, or three gates on each side. There's 12 gates for the 12 apostles, and there's other
9 things too that relate to the Israelites.
10 Now people are going to say, well, that's racist, why are you going to have the white race running
11 everybody? And obviously that's who it's going to be there. Now, that's going to twist the nose on a
12 lot of people when they understand that, but I guess it's so different that people will be totally
13 blown away. They won't recall what went on on this planet, in this life. That will not be in a memory.
14 There will be no memory of that. I understand, though, that there will be some recognition of
15 people by each other. Now, I don't know where it says that or what, but that's the general feeling I
16 get from reading things. Now you have to remember that the absolute pinnacle of existence in this
17 universe will be to be a son of God, living with the creator of the universe forever.
18
19 Now this planet, to handle the city of God, is going to have to increase in volume. People are
20 telling me that it's going to have to increase about 360 times in size . That, in a way, is beyond
21 what we can visualize. But, on the other hand, who is going to be residing there? This big, this big
22 planet, this big city is the one and only creator of the universe and his son. They are the
23 government of God, along with the Holy Spirit, and so it's going to be a big place. He says there
24 will be no more sea
25
26 I've gone on quite a few cruises. I was mesmerized by sitting out on the Lido deck and looking at
27 the water. Here, we're going through all this water , water. Where did it all come from, like, how did
28 it all get here? It would have to be created by God Almighty in one big swoop. And when you
29 consider that water is such an element, we take it for granted. Man, do we ever? But it can be gas,
30 it can be ice solid and it can be liquid. And we're made out of it. We are both 70% water. We're
31 basically a walking blob of water and fat and minerals and whatever else in a body that God
32 created and made, a system to replicate over and over and over. An actual system. Bunch of kinds
33 of things, not cells, they're like little pieces of motors and this and that and all kinds of things that
34 run this cell.
35

1 You know, it is so amazing, I guess, and I'm starting to believe that that is what's going to generate
2 all the interest and the beautiful living expectations that people will have forever in a forever
3 universe. They'll never be bored anymore, ever, because God is unlimited. You know, like he says
4 things like the mind of man has never even dreamt of or considered what God has planned for
5 them. Now, that just says it in a nutshell and what he's saying is that you're not going to be bored,
6 and what a promise. Now, when you read and hear something like that and you look around and
7 you listen and you see people who say Don't believe in God, don't believe in this. Now we've got a
8 whole generation that says we don't believe in God. That's sad, that's sad, that's very sad. I mean
9 my family has gone that way, absolutely gone that way, and it just gripes me to no end to think that
10 I grew up, got married, had three children and, as far as I can tell, they don't believe in anything.
11 My wife had a big influence in that she would not believe in Jesus Christ or God, even though she
12 was involved in a situation where we had an actual miracle happen in our family To our youngest
13 son, who was four years old, got diseased with blood disease of some kind, black marks up and
14 down his legs, all over the place and the bottom of his feet, and he couldn't walk and crying, you
15 know. The specialist said well, you got two weeks to live, that's it. You better take pictures of him
16 while you can. He's gonna just go down right away.
17
18 It was Friday in Red Deer, Alberta. He was 4 years old. So I'll just tell you the rest of the story now.
19 When I started it, we were in to see this specialist. He gave us the news that our son, Jeff, was
20 going to die within about two weeks. Because he was small, he had a small blood base I mean not
21 very much so this was going to spread through his blood within two weeks and he would die. And
22 he suggested we take him up to the hospital and they would do whatever they could there. So we
23 took him up to the hospital and I remember walking down the hallway and the nurses
24 came walking towards us and there were tears in their eyes. You know they knew what was going
25 on.
26
27 Well, Friday night, my wife just collapsed when he told her that and she was beside herself and he
28 quickly whipped out some pills of some kind to give her medication to calm her down. And it
29 calmed her down, didn't give me anything. I just sat there looking and it didn't give me anything.
30 Now I took the boy up to the hospital, dropped him off at the hospital and headed back to Rocky
31 Mountain House, 50 miles, and my wife's just staring out the window in the car and just had no
32 idea, she was just out of it. I was driving along and I was not feeling very happy. I mean, now I'll
33 tell you what I did.
34
35 Leaving Red Deer and on the left-hand side was a building and it was a liquor store. So I pulled
36 into the liquor store, went in and bought a Mickey, of rye, pulled out on the highway and I went
37 again, and I kind of nursed that Mickey the 50 miles into Rocky Mountain House. By the time I got
38 there it was gone. I just drank it up and that, I guess, sort of helped me settle down a little bit.
39

1 When we got home, the first thing she did was run in the house and started pulling pictures out
2 from everywhere she could find and dumping them on the bed. I'm going through trying to find
3 pictures of Jeff. Well, I told her, I said look, God does, say that if two of you believe and ask for
4 something, that God will grant it. I said do you believe that? Yes, yes. Well, I thought I don't know if
5 you do or not, but I said let's do that. So we got down beside the bed, put our hands on the bed
6 and we both said please, god, we're both in agreement. We would ask that you would interfere
7 with this thing and save our son from the terrible disease that he has. We ask it in Jesus' name,
8 amen. And that was it.
9 I got up and I went down to the shop I had in Rocky Mountain House. I had this building and in the
10 building I had a dry cleaning plant. I was working for a pipeline company. I had a little office down
11 there with a phone in it and I went in there. This was like about 6.30 at night, it was getting dark
12 and I had basically a little cubby hole office just with a kind of a bit of a desk thing in there under
13 the stairway. I went in there, got on the phone.
14
15 His name was Max Solbrecken, in Edmonton, Alberta. He was a fiery preacher, I guess you'd say.
16 Anyway, I remember hearing him saying he was having this big crusade in the Jubilee Auditorium
17 in Edmonton and I thought it was that day and I looked up the number. I called the Jubilee
18 Auditorium, asked for Max Solbrecken and she said yes, he's here, I'll get him for you. I just sat
19 there and I started to shake. I was really nervous.
20 He came on the phone and said what can I do for you? So I told him. I said my son's in Red Deer
21 and the doctor said he's only got two weeks to live and I would ask you to pray for him if there's
22 any possibility of that. And he says yes. He said I will do that. We'll have 700 people here. He said
23 in about the next hour there will be 700 people here in the Jubilee Auditorium and he said I will ask
24 them all to pray for your son, Jeffrey, in the Red Deer Hospital.
25 And said you have to get down on your knees and follow me and say these words and do exactly
26 as I say. So I said yes, yes, yes, got down on my knees in the dark and I started to get really
27 emotional. I started to sob and he said the words , and I just repeated what he said and shaking
28 and sobbing, and I just said thank you very much. And he said all right, god bless you we will take
29 it from here. And I got up from there, I went home. I don't think I said anything to my wife.
30
31 The next morning I told her **that our other** two kids were staying somewhere else. I said you better
32 come with me. It's pretty hard for you to sit home alone here. I said I have to go to work. So she
33 said, okay, got in the pickup and we drove around the oil fields and, oh man, it must have been
34 Saturday morning. Yes, it was Saturday morning. And as she rode around with me and I
35 remember, around noon like it was a signal, and yet I don't know if it was or not we were driving
36 around in the oil field and I remember turning and driving sort of southwest in a direction and into
37 this tank farm and as I drove in, the clouds just opened up and the sun just blasted right there and

1 it was just bright, And I looked up at it and I thought, oh I said I think that's a sign that Jeff's going
2 to be okay. And I said to her you know what? He's going to be okay and that's all I said.
3 We went home, went to bed. On Sunday morning at about quarter to ten, the phone rang and
4 there was this woman from the hospital in Red Deer and she said you can come and pick up your
5 son. He's fine. That's all she said, and I just said thank you very much. We drove into Red Deer.
6 We went up the two floors where we had left him and I was walking down this hallway. This
7 specialist doctor came walking towards me and he just looked the other way and wouldn't look me
8 in the eye, just walked by. We went in and they brought Jeff out. All the black marks were gone, he
9 was fine, we took him home and that was it.
10
11 Now there's no coincidences here, none, and I have thanked God many times for this, many times.
12   So later on, I'm going to talk about the idea that people can have access to the Creator of the
13 Universe, that you know, the most powerful entity in the whole universe, the Creator God. We don't
14 really know. We are built in His image, that's all we know and that we will become sons at some
15 stage and that he's made arrangements for somebody to cover for us, because we could not keep
16   his laws and he had to have it that way because we had to voluntarily want to be his son. We
17 couldn't have any other way to do it. So I'm pretty glad that God is in charge of things. That's for
18 sure, and so should you be. You know we take a lot of things for granted, that's for sure. totally for
19 granted. Anyway, that's it for tonight. I'd like to say God bless you and keep you. Thank you very
20   much.

21
22
23
24
25
26
27
28
29   **Timeless Values: Navigating Life Lessons**
30   **from a Farm in Alberta**
31
32
33

1

Chapter 2

3

4 Have you ever wondered how childhood experiences in nature could shape a lifelong journey of
5 spirituality and purpose? Join us as we explore a heartwarming tale of growing up on a farm in
6 Alberta, where a deep connection to the natural world intertwined with family life and faith. Our
7 host reflects on pivotal moments that defined his youth, from the profound realization of his
8 purpose at 15 to treasured memories of listening to boxing matches with his father and enjoying
9 the simple, yet delicious, meals prepared by his mother on a wood stove.

10

11 Step back in time for a nostalgic look at rural life, filled with both thrilling adventures and everyday
12 routines that painted a vivid picture of a close-knit community. Experience the excitement and risks
13 of galloping down railroad tracks and the communal joy of bobsleigh rides to town during the
14 winter. Feel the transformative impact of electricity's arrival on the farm, bringing modern
15 conveniences like the refrigerator that eased household chores. Relive the spirit of family
16 gatherings, weekend picnics, and carefree flatbed truck rides that defined the host's childhood.

17

18 Discover the industrious spirit of family farm life, where economic challenges were met with
19 resilience and creativity. Our host shares personal stories of hard work, like milking cows before
20 school and repairing equipment in the fields, and recounts an inspiring encounter with a school
21 superintendent that led to a pursuit of higher education and entrepreneurial success. Hear about
22 strategic business decisions and innovative management practices, such as profit-sharing, that
23 played key roles in expanding the family business. This episode is a treasure trove of life lessons
24 and timeless values gleaned from 90 years of a well-lived life.

25

26 Well, good afternoon. It's Arlo Johnson in Vernon, British Columbia, on the 10th of June. So I'd like
27 to discuss the idea of nature, and I think you know we overlook nature as we're growing up. We
28 see something, oh there, it looks nice there and what's that? Oh, isn't that a wonderful thing there?
29 But that's all. We kind of just gloss over it. Actually, nature is the handiwork of God, almighty and
30 Jesus as creator. Now you know, to look at nature and try to figure out how that all works is just
31 amazing, I've talked about water, plain water, how amazing water is, what kind of a substance that
32 is and how God could use 70% of that to make a human being to wander around here on the
33 earth. And I've been on it now for 90 years. This body has been sloshing around for 90 years fixing
34 itself and healing itself from all kinds of things. It's a vehicle. You know, it really is just a vehicle for
35 people to navigate around on this planet. Navigate around this planet to work, to build things too.
36 You know, the thing is, I don't like when I hear people say it's my body and I can do whatever I

1 want with it. No, that's not true, and you can look at that any way you like. It's not a true deal, it's
2 BS. You didn't create anything. Your life was given to you, your spirit was given to you, your body
3 was given to you and it's given to you for a purpose. A purpose I realized when I was about 15
4 years old. I remember standing out in the yard one time. I forget what I was doing. But I was just
5 standing out there and all of a sudden this thought came over me: what am I doing here? Why am
6 I here? And I'm standing out there kind of looking around at things, and all of a sudden I said to
7 myself I realized that I was here to make a decision about God and about life and about what to
8 believe. I knew that at 15 years old. I remember that very plainly. You know, you think out of a
9 whole 90 years that you remember this. But I remember that very plainly. And the thing is, the
10 reason to believe things is, or it should be, by example or truth or whatever. You know you see
11 what, how this works, how that works. How did that get here? How did that work? And then you
12 say to yourself God must have created it. And here he's created this wonderful thing for us to use.
13 And I remember while I grew up on a farm. Yeah, on a farm in Alberta and I think that was a good
14 place to grow up.
15 I had two very wonderful parents. I could never have found a mother and a father more dedicated
16 to my benefit than it seems like they treated me so well. Never once did my dad ever say anything
17 to me like you know anger or anything else like that, or you should do this and quit doing that. No,
18 nothing, never, nothing. Sometimes he just sits and looks at me and I get very uneasy and I
19 thought, why are you just looking at me like that? And they treated me, you know, way beyond
20 what I expected or deserved, and you know it's a pretty nice thing when somebody does that, I
21 guess. But I realized later on that I could never have had two people more dedicated to my well-
22 being than those two. They were very good to me and they weren't fancy people, just a great
23 Father and Mother.
24
25 Dad wasn't a big man really, but he was like broad, wide, he had wide shoulders and he had
26 biceps 21 and a half inches. I'll never forget that, laying on the floor listening to the Joe Louis
27 heavyweight boxing champions of the world going on and they're giving the specs and the size of
28 the fighters. And they got down to Joe Lewis and they said, well, Joe Lewis has 21 and a half inch
29 biceps. So we got all excited and we went and got a tape measure and we measured dad's biceps
30 because he was laying there listening to the fight too. He liked listening to that. His biceps were 21
31 and a half. He was a big, strong guy and we were pretty excited about that. Dad's biceps as big
32 Joe Louis world champion. Well, those days are really gone.
33 You know it's sad, but those days are really gone. Those were days of, I'd say, innocence. I
34 remember when we didn't have any electric power and my mom cooked everything on a wood
35 stove and cooked everything fresh and new every day because we didn't have a fridge and it was
36 good. I remember coming home from school and running in the door about 3: 30, and she'd have

1 some simple things on, like sometimes it would be a plate with fresh white bread on it and then
2 covered with sour cream and strawberries. Oh man, you know we thought that was great, you
3 know that's all it was, but we really liked that.
4 When you get to be my age, you start to, you know, reminisce about things, and you think about
5 the history and what goes on. Sometimes I just think about my life. For instance, My dad gave me
6 a horse when I was six years old. That horse lived 27 years. He was a three-quarter size horse. He
7 wasn't a bighorse, he was part something, I don't what, but he was a stubborn thing. You know, he
8 was good, he was. He could run like the dickens.
9 I was going to a school called Armena. It was about two and a half miles from where we were
10 living and these other boys in my class had Hamiltonians and they were race horses.Their dad had
11 bought them Hamiltonian ponies. Well, they weren't just ponies, they were race horses. And we
12 would go down the road half a mile to the north and then half a mile straight west and then we turn
13 off. Well, when we got to the corner of the road that went half a mile straight west, that was the
14 racetrack, half mile racetrack. And of course they just look at each other, look at me, and they'd
15 kick the ribs of their horses and they'd start riding as fast as they could. And I was on Tony, my
16 horse and I, just basically just let him run and he laid his ears right back on his head and he'd run
17 and he'd get to the half mile before them every time and just stop dead there and head north at a
18 slow rate. And they used to just hate it that they couldn't beat him. And here he was a smaller
19 horse and whatever, but he just wouldn't let them beat him. Period, yeah, and that was that. That
20 was an eye-opener for me.That a smaller horse could be so determined.
21 I remember riding down the railroad track with my sister behind me and I had kind of one-inch nails
22 in my heels so I could use them like spurs and I was riding full gallop down the railroad track. Now,
23 when I think about that, I think what a stupid thing to do. If he had stumbled or something, we
24 could have been killed. I **didn't do** it too many times, I think that was stupid, stupid thing to do. But
25 you know, in a person's lifetime, if you were to count up the stupid things that a person does, you
26 could write about ten books. It really takes a long time to get any semblance of wisdom. You know,
27 don't do this or that will happen
28
29 I remember going to town six miles in the winter with a team of horses in a bobsleigh, full of hay
30 and grain and stuff like that and a seat up in the front where Dad would sit there with his big buffalo
31 coat on In the wintertime. We'd go into town. It would take like two and a half hours for the horses
32 to go the six miles and we had all the hay in there and everything. And we go like you know, eight,
33 nine o'clock in the morning, get to town, maybe about 10: 30 and when we got to town there was a
34 big area like a parking lot for horses and sleighs and box full boxes and I would. I can't remember
35 offhand but I know there would be about 30 different teams of horses in this parking lot thing. It
36 had a wall built around it and people would pull in to the lot, tie up their horses, get the hay out, put

it out for the horses, because you know we're gonna be there a couple of hours and all us kids, you know we were like eight, nine, eight, nine, ten years old, eleven maybe. Oh, we were all chasing each other around, playing games and doing stuff and, later on I guess we'd be in the restaurant and get something to eat there.

You know it was a day on the town and we'd get groceries and stuff like that and we'd get them right just before we went home and we'd put them in the bobsleigh and then piled all kinds of hay and straw around it to hopefully keep it from freezing until we got home. And of course it took another two and a half hours of plodding along and we'd run behind the sleigh or we'd hang onto it or, you know, get bored and come in and lay in the hay and then get up and run again. Yeah, get home, get the groceries in the house as soon as possible as it was starting to freeze. But you know a totally different way of life, totally. And the difference, the big difference was well, when we got power, things changed big time. Farm Electric came around and they just went mile after mile after mile with a power line and then into the yard and I don't know if they brought it right up to the house, but I think they maybe did.

And then we had to get somebody to wire the house. Everything was wired on the outside, you know, it wasn't inside Wires running around the walls all over the place. And then we got lights. No heat or anything but lights used a wood stove. We got a fridge, the first fridge we ever had, and that changed a whole lot of things for mom.She could save things for the next day. Every day Fresh bread would be on the table by noon and you know I often wondered about that amount. I remember we had like half a beef hanging on a granary, especially in the fall winter time. You know, just hung there, we'd go out and chop a big chunk off and bring it in and roast it, cook it, do whatever, and you know it was pretty fresh and that's what's been going on all winter.

Now the thing is when you, when you grow up like that, you know it's a different thing. When I was growing up, family was everything. It was totally everything. We had a big family and there were families all around us. Some of my relatives and others were a little farther away but like on the weekends for sure, we went to their place and it was a picnic party kind of thing. They would come to our place, all kinds of cousins and stuff around, and that went on all the time, every single weekend. We never went anywhere. We didn't go anywhere to see anything else. We went, hung around with our relatives, cousins, aunts, uncles, had a big picnic, spent the day there, and came home at 5, 6 o'clock at night.

This one uncle had a BA bulk station dealership and he had this flatbed, I think, one-ton truck and you know he'd haul barrels of gas on it but he'd come around with that on, you know, like Saturday morning early and we'd all pile on it, just pile on it, pile on the truck at the back and away we'd go to the lake and you know it could be quite a few of us on a flat deck and I don't think it had any

1 sides on it either. But we didn't worry about that. Nobody fell off. He didn't go very fast either. He
2 went, you know, at a pretty reasonable speed.
3
4 And you know, I remember coming back from the lake, we lived south three miles south of the of
5 the Lake, which was a provincial park deal, and we're coming home this one afternoon, on a
6 saturday afternoon or was it sunday, I'm not sure about three o'clock, and my mother and her
7 sister decided they should stop. They thought they saw a bunch of I don't know what kind of
8 berries it was. But they got Albin to stop along the side of the road, kind of on a corner, and pull off
9 and they grabbed these buckets and the way they went right through this fence and into this guy's
10 property , and they're whispering. You know, I hope they don't mind. You know we shouldn't really
11 be here. And me and my cousin Norman watched them go in there. We got off and we went
12 around where they couldn't see us, went through the bush and crawled in behind some big trees
13 and we watched and we listened to them. They were squeaking through these fences with their
14 dresses and stuff and they said, oh, look here. Oh, here's a whole bunch here. Oh, man, this is
15 good, isn't it? We took a little rock or something and we'd throw it and it would land somewhere,
16 just pass them and then say what was that? What was that? And then we wait a little while and
17 they look around. They couldn't see anything. They started picking again. We'd throw another rock.
18 they know we're here, we've gotta get out of here. Oh, and they started running with their pail
19 buckets and berries spilling and running and going through the fence too fast. The barbed wire
20 fence was catching their dresses, ripping them, and Norman and I ran around the outside, got
21 back on the truck and were sitting waiting for them and they came rushing in and they said we've
22 gotta get out of here. They know we're here. And Norman and I just sat and we had a very hard
23 time keeping our mouths shut not laughing, they didn't know and it lasted for quite a while. Oh,
24 that was fun.
25
26 The business of families and family life, family farm life. You know, I didn't realize it growing up on
27 a farm but we had to rely on that farm. In our case we had two sections, 320 acres. A lot of people
28 just had 160. And they were raising a family and building houses, barns, and all kinds of stuff. And
29 anyway we had to produce every single stick of everything from that farm, whether it was grain,
30 hogs, chickens, eggs, milk, selling pigs, selling cattle. In the fall grain sell some grain, but most of it
31 we'd keep half of it for feed. And it all went on all year long.
32 Certain times you'd sell something and you'd get enough money to do something. You'd get a few
33 hundred dollars At that time. That was basically all you'd get. You know, you could sell ten pigs
34 and maybe make 150 bucks on the whole works, but what I'm getting at there was no pension,
35 there was no workman's thing or any kind of government supplement or help None, none at all,
36 whether it was for health or anything. You went to town, you paid the doctor cash right there. The
37 doctor seemed to be doing fine and he didn't charge that much. You know, maybe it was 15 or 20
38 dollars to stitch up a finger or do this or get something for a bad cold.
39

And you know, we had to be an economic unit absolutely on our own. We had to figure out how to do that too. Now there's lots of times the boys that grew up on a farm like that in Alberta or Saskatchewan, They were way better equipped to work in a place where you had to, you know, use your head and figure things out, way better than people living in a city, just living in a home apartment, and I think that's true. Well, I remember having to figure out how to get unstuck or the tractor would have something wrong and I had to fix it out on the field on my own, get it going again. And you know, you had to rely on yourself, you had to figure things out, and that made it like a school of hard knocks. There's no doubt about that. That's gone. Yeah, the farms nowadays are so mechanized and everything it's a different story, but it's still got its reliance workshop experience. You have to. You still have to get things working and going, and guessing about the weather and whether we can do it now or wait till tomorrow or, you know, get rained out, hailed out all kinds of things.

Yeah, I remember having to get up in the morning and go and milk cows before I went to school. Well, I just had to do it. I don't know why but I was always getting an A If you were really good. You got an H for honors, b, c, whatever. I never had anything less than A's and B's and H's and A's and B's and H's. And in fact last year I was in school I got most half H's and half A's and that was it. I think that was grade nine. And last year I actually went to school and I remember the superintendent of schools for the Camrose District, the largest district, came out in July. I think in the middle of July or something came out to the farm and wanted to see me.

I guess dad told him well, he's out, he's raking hay. Actually, right now on the farm, you can drive right through the road you can take. So here he comes, driving across the fields in this big blue sedan. I thought who is coming out here? And I remember sitting on this rake with this team of horses and looking at them. And he pulls up, gets out and he says hi, my name is Mr Robinson. I'm superintendent of schools from school district number 22. Oh, is that right? What do you want? He said I've come out here to talk to you about going to university. And I thought I didn't know about that. He said, with your marks and your stuff that you've had we've looked at your records. We really suggest strongly that you keep going to school and get into university. And I thought, oh my God, I'm still sitting on this hayrake looking at him. And he said you know, Arlo, if there's anything we can do for you, please let us know and let's hope we'll see you this fall. Goodbye, And he goes and I'm sitting there watching him go and dust flying up in the field and there he goes, it disappears, and I'm sitting there and I'm like a big dummy. I'm thinking to myself if I'm that smart, I don't need to go to school anymore, you know, and I thought, oh man, I thought later, you idiot.

I did take some courses later on, in Mount Royal College and in Red Deer. It was a business administration course and the whole thing was, Mount Royal College was a hands-on deal. You had to come up with a project that you could actually build or start and you had to be able to run it. When your course was through. You had to get the full report on everything, how you were going to do everything, and I had looked at dry cleaning plants in Rocky Mountain House because there wasn't any. And you know Rocky Mountain House was getting to be a good-sized town and I went through everything. You know buying this and the cost of this and how I'm going to do everything, where I'm going to get the money from. And other guys there were some two or three of them who went together on a project to build a big hotel and they did. They built a big hotel and others had other projects and I got an A plus in my course.

I started small with a little unit in a furniture store and I had hired a woman to run it. People would bring their dry cleaning in and run it through this automatic machine. But that didn't work out very well. So I got a hold of McGraw Edison in the United States and they had a deal. They were promoting a thing called one-hour martinizing. That was their whole deal. And that was a one hour Martinizing you take it in and one hour later you can get it back. And that was their deal. And they had a handbook about one inch thick. And their deal was you buy the equipment from us, we'll finance it for you and you'll have to put it in, install it, and you'll need, you know, 1500 to 2000 square feet for sure. And so I thought about it and I signed up for it. Big truck came with all these big machines and boilers and everything, and I ended up with a full plant in Rocky Mountain House. Now the boys that I hung around with two of them were plumbers and one was a car dealer. They saw that this one-hour martinizing was a pretty good deal. I was making money. It had said exactly what size sign to have and to do this, they even guaranteed that if you followed their book one, if there's more than one dry cleaning plant in this town, it will go broke and you will survive. And that's what happened.

We went to Calgary and we signed up with an outfit called Marathon Realty, a branch of CNR who had railroad stations in every town downtown. They were phasing them out, but they had that land right downtown and they were converting this into shopping centers, downtown shopping centers. So we went to Calgary and we went up to this big building and it was a CN tower.. It was their company and me and Clayton, who was a car dealer, we went there to negotiate. We wanted to negotiate for a business spot. You know, a commercial business spot in Camrose and one in Stettler.

Anyway, they were right down at the end of Main Street. If you were on Main Street and looked right down, you'd look at our sign 4 by 20, one hour martinizing In Camrose. If you looked down Main Street, you'd see our sign right dead in the middle of the street Because the buildings went crossways to the end of the street. We went up into this big building and these people are very, you know, nice.
Oh, hello, come on in. Uh, yes, could we get you anything to drink, and would you like coffee? And I said, well, I guess we could have coffee. That's not what we came for. We want to talk to somebody about leasing in Stettler and in Camrose in your new shopping centers. Oh well, let's

1 just talk about it. We'll go to this office for our coffee. We had a map out of the building , on the wall
2 showing all the different spots in the building and how soon they're going to be ready and they're
3 working on them.
4 And we went up and we said we'd like this one right here in Stettler and we'd like that one right
5 there in Camrose. Oh, yes, that's a good choice, you know, yeah. And I said, how much is that
6 going to be? How much are you going to be renting for? And they said, well, that's going to be, you
7 know so much per sq ft for it . And I said what does that come to? Well, for Stettler, I think it's $265
8 a month. And I said, and what about Camrose? Well, that's a little bit bigger and it's a bigger town
9 and everything. So that'll be about $350 of rent for those units, I see, and I just looked at Clayton
10
11 and I said you know what? Do you have a check with you? And he feels around and says, yeah, I
12 do, I do have one. Well, I said let's leave him a check for $615 total.
13 It wasn't that much, it's definitely this much for unit number 22 and unit number 8. And we gave
14 him this check and the guy says well, I don't know, I don't think I could actually take checks right
15 now. I mean, this is a little early yet, you know. Oh no, I said that's fine, you got a text there, you go
16 ahead. And I said also, we will want 10 years, 10 years at a fixed price, at this price, with the
17 option, our option, to extend it for another 10 years at the same price. Oh, I see, I said, remember
18 now, 10 years plus 10 year option at our choice.
19
20 About 2 months later I got this big envelope, heavy envelope, and two big copies of leases Black
21 covered deals fancy things. Open it up, oh man, it was about 40 pages long each one and I looked
22 at it and I said,being the president of this company that we formed Plaza Cleaners, so I had to sign
23 it and send it back, and I did. I just signed it, president Plaza Cleaners.Kept one copy and I sent
24 the other one back to Calgary.
25 We went to Stettler first, put that plant in, got it going, and hired a manager in Stettler who had
26 been running grain elevators, a fairly young guy. I told him you go ahead and run this, it's your
27 baby to run and we'll do profit sharing with you. Oh, okay, that's better than the grain elevator. He
28 got in there and he was running that thing, you know, like he was in the Chamber of Commerce .
29 And he was promoting everything, doing real good. Went to Camrose, got that in and got it
30 running, hired another manager there and he was not quite as good, but he was pretty good and
31 had them both running right
32
33 About 6 months later Marathon Realty sent us a letter requesting we discuss the terms of the
34 renewal as they felt they could not live with these terms.I wrote back and said that we were quite
35 satisfied and thanked them for their interest. Never heard from them again.
36

Navigating the Ninetieth Year: A Nonagenarian's Musings on Faith, Family, and the Fathomless Divine

Chapter 3

When the candles on the birthday cake number 90, the stories they illuminate are rich with the wisdom of years and the patina of history. Our latest episode features Arlo Johnson, a nonagenarian from Vernon, BC, who shares his life's reflections during a heartfelt birthday tribute. Arlo offers candid insights on the era he's lived through, including his traditional beliefs and values, which sometimes clash with today's societal norms, particularly regarding LGBTQ+ rights. It's a poignant conversation that not only celebrates Arlo's milestone but also delves into the complexities of reconciling deep-seated faith with the love for one's family and the shifts in cultural perceptions.

Consider for a moment the vast tapestry of human existence, woven with the lives of over 100 billion souls who have graced this Earth. In our episode, we ponder this immense number and the divine criteria that might govern the celestial reckoning of such lives. Arlo muses on the nature of good, evil, and the incomprehensible aspects of a divine being, all while expressing gratitude for the simplicity and routine of daily existence. Join us as we navigate these philosophical waters and extend an open-hearted invitation to reflect, appreciate, and partake in the blessings we share with our listeners

Well, good evening. It's Arlo Johnson from Vernon, bc. On April the 25th at 9.30 pm. Spring is here. It's starting to warm up a little bit, not too much yet, but it's nice to see the spring is here, the leaves are coming out, things are turning. It's nice to see the spring is here, the leaves are coming out and things are turning. I was going to mention a little bit about the last few days.

April 25th my birthday was on April 22nd. I turned 90 on Monday, April 22nd and I don't know if birthday business started like on the 21st on Sunday cakes and stuff and whatever from some people on my birthday actually I didn't really. Oh, yes, Sunday, the day before my birthday, my sister arranged for cousins and my son and his girlfriend and I guess that's about it. Four or five people came over here to the Vernon Rest Home, brought a cake and cards and stuff and

1 whatever. Well, which was nice, I guess. Then actually on oh, I forget what day it was, but the rest
2 home here had a deal for people with birthdays and got cards and stuff there. Then I think it was
3 on 23rd, oh, yes, 23rd Then I went out to Desert Cove and had a big cake and stuff out there and
4 people you know wishing well. I'd drive down the street and people would run out to the street
5 waving at me and saying happy birthday to our own residents, you know. And walking through the
6 main hall, people were waving at me. I thought how the heck do they know it was my birthday? But
7 what it is is. I guess it's a bit of a milestone. You know, I should have never planned, I didn't think
8 of myself being 90 years old and it, you know, just crept up on me. I'm now yet 90 years old and
9 out of style To the world. Well, I can't help that.
10
11 There's things that have affected me quite a bit on the not good side, due to the fact that I've
12 grown up with certain beliefs and whatever, and one of them had to do with growing up with certain
13 beliefs and whatever, and one of them had to do with with what I was taught and all the things I
14 went to catechism and Sunday school and church and whatever for 60 years, and what I've
15 studied church and whatever for 60 years and what I've studied since and whatever else. One of
16 the things that has happened in this world is that homosexual has become more prevalent. It's
17 been around for a long time, I don't know, throughout history, and it's a thing that is very, very,
18 what would you say, abhorrent to the creator of the universe, god and Jesus. And they are
19 basically creators of the universe, God and Jesus, and they basically included in the list of things
20 that keep people out of the city of God, or the book of life of Jesus Christ, along with many other
21 things, along with many other things. But it was bad enough that God actually destroyed two cities
22 and just destroyed them forever, and I've always kind of, you know, I have not liked the idea of
23 that.
24
25 And then for people to say, well, it's their choice, you know, well, of course it's their choice, but it
26 doesn't make it right. The thing is, it seems to me so devilish that it promotes a lie. You know, gay,
27 is it a gay lifestyle? Gay, that's not what I thought gay meant when I grew up, and the gay lifestyle
28 is couched in all kinds of love and this and that. That is another lie.
29
30 People, they try to pretend to get married man with man and woman with woman. That doesn't
31 work out. You see all the flashy things they do and pretend that this man is not my wife and you
32 know, that just grates me. I know that that's a lie. Why should you promote and want to promote a
33 lie? And the thing that bothers me is that if people support and encourage gay lifestyles and
34 whatever, I think they're going to be classed in the same boat as an homosexual and God is going

1 to say I don't know, you, don't go to come around me, and why would I want that to happen to
2 somebody that is, you know nothing worse than that you can. You know you don't want that to
3 happen to somebody. Now people get mad at you because you don't want it to happen. You're
4 supposed to accept it. That's wrong. You can't accept something like that. It's not that there are not
5 other things that are just as bad and God abhors. I know that. But why pick on one and try to
6 glorify it? And that's what they do. They don't try to glorify people getting drunk. They don't try to
7 glorify, you know, all kinds of things murder and robbery and killing and whatever. Well, they do in
8 some cases, but not like that. They don't try to glorify it.
9
10 I'd say that, you know, take the rainbow colors and use them as their symbol. The rainbow colors
11 were given by God as a promise to the world. So that's caused problems. I've had to live with that.
12 Now I've been ostracized over that with my own family. They don't want to talk to me anymore
13 because they figure I'm biased and whatever. That's too bad. I hate it because I know it's wrong to
14 do that.
15
16 And the thing is I didn't change. They changed, not me. You know you don't live 90 years and see
17 everything that's going on in 90 years. You know it's a fair amount of time and realize that in the
18 last 10, 15 years between abortion and homosexual and gay and whatever, I mean that's been a
19 big push. Now it's transgender and this, and that All perverted stuff perverted the natural human
20 beings, and they glorify that. What it amounts to is and I've said this quite a few times is it's a
21 prediction that Isaiah made and that was who knows how long that was. That's thousands of years
22 ago. But anyway, he wrote in the book of Isaiah. It's in the book that when good is evil and evil is
23 good, you know you are living in the last days. Well, that's exactly where we are now. Only a lot of
24 people overlook it, plain overlook it and say it's all just, you know modern times and ha ha ha, isn't
25 that great, That's bad. That is so bad.
26
27 Why in the world would a person or people willingly and I say willingly put themselves in a situation
28 where they're going to be barred from a second, wonderful, perfect life forever? This life's earth
29 deal cycle that we're born into actually makes us great cosmic travelers. I'm going to figure out
30 how many miles I've traveled since April 22, 1934. And I'm going to have to sit down and figure it
31 out because I know that I'm revolving, the Earth is revolving, which I'm on, and we're at about,
32 most likely, 1,000 miles per hour. It's 1,200 at the equator, but we're quite a ways from the equator,
33 so we're going a little slower on the curve. Now that's 1,000 miles an hour and I'm traveling around
34 the sun through space at 68,000 miles per hour. Now I don't know exactly how many miles it is

1 around the sun. One year trip. I've been doing that for 90 years and that makes a lot of mileage.
2 That's what you call high mileage. I guess, instead of somebody who lives a long time, I could say
3 that well, they're high mileage, which would be true.
4
5 We are born into this world, created Bang like that Between a male sperm and a female egg.
6 We're created A mystery of mysteries of how it all works and it all happens in an instant, everything
7 that's going to require that life take place, Now that comes with only one thing that survives that,
8 and that is the spirit that God puts in you when you are conceived and it leaves you when you die
9 and goes back to God who gave it. It most likely carries a full record of everything you've ever
10 done and I think that's what it's there for. You are created, put together cell by cell, flying together
11 at high speed. In fact, most likely, you know thousands of cells an hour being produced and going
12 here and going there, and then to end up like, like I am, 90 years later, still going, the body is still
13 producing stuff and looking after, healing itself and replacing itself.
14
15 Now the thing is and I knew this well, I knew this and it came to me like I don't know why, but it
16 came to me like. I don't know why, but it came to me like when I was 15 years old. I remember I
17 don't know what day it was. But I remember that I had this thought that came over me that what
18 was I doing here on this planet? And I realized that I was here to make a decision, and so was
19 everyone else, because I realized then that people lived and died and whatever, and didn't stay
20 here forever.
21
22 So what it belongs to, what it ends up being, is that we are given a life. We didn't buy it, we didn't
23 get it from Walmart or the hardware store. We were given a life, we were given a vehicle, a body to
24 live in. It's not ours, we didn't produce it, we didn't create it.
25
26 And all of a sudden, about nine months later, we come out of this womb that the woman carries
27 and we pop open her eyes and take a look and say what is this? And we see people looking at us.
28 This you know. And we see people looking at us and we don't know who they are and we don't
29 know anything. Basically, maybe there might be some sort of slight instinct to know. I mean, we
30 know that we have to suckle and have food and we know what we have to eat and if we don't eat,
31 we'll bawl and holler and cry to get it. You know things like that, survival things but we have to
32 learn everything and you know we're kind of slow learners. It takes us a while to. It takes us a year
33 or so to even learn how to walk. Now the thing is there's people dying. I think there's , One person

1 who dies every two seconds or something like that. That in the world, and that's around the clock,
2 24 hours a day, seven days a week.
3
4 Now, we came into this world as a gift. We were given a body and a life and we are here to make
5 a decision about who did this for us and why. We should be grateful. Some do, some don't. Now,
6 when we leave, we leave with the same amount as we came with Nothing. In fact, we don't even
7 have a thing . Our spirit has gone back to God and we're just a shell, just a wet spot on the rug.
8
9 But anyway, you know, that's a fact. You can't argue that, nobody can argue that. You can argue
10 and win, because that is exactly what happens to everyone. We come and we leave, and the only
11 thing we are capable of doing is acknowledging that God created us and that he sent his son to
12 save us because we couldn't keep his law and that was God's plan. In the long run, that was his
13 plan. The only way he could create sons was for someone else to take the fall for them, because
14 they couldn't quite do it. And being here, made in the image of God, and God fine-tunes the rest
15 later, because you know to cultivate somebody to be your son forever and to think like you and do
16 like you and have the mind of God and whatever, hopefully.
17
18 Now, I think the worst possible thing is that people want to believe that there's nothing or and they
19 do it in full realization that there's no hope for them, none Zero. And I think about that so much. I
20 think that what a total waste it is for a person to live on this planet for 50 to 100 years, or whatever
21 it is, and just plain fail, fail to do one simple thing that God wanted acknowledgement, that he had
22 made arrangements to save you. Now human beings are in such a class that we're most likely
23 rated way higher than we realized by God Almighty. It's because he created us in his own image
24 and from a little bit of bits and pieces here and there. It appears to me that the angels in heaven
25 and spiritual beings are basically not jealous but in awe of human beings, because they are a
26 spark of the eternal God. They are created in the image and everything of God. Nobody else is
27 created in the image of God.
28
29 That God created and arranged the universe in such a way that was compatible for life on Earth
30 for his children, and to change the universe around afterwards to create an eternal kingdom where
31 his children would reside with him. Which means he said he's going to create a new heaven and a
32 new earth, new heavens that's a lot to change and a new earth. This earth is going to be dissolved
33 and redone, and I mentioned this before. The city of God that God is creating, or Jesus is creating.
34 Jesus said I'm going to prepare a place for you. So it's obvious he's the builder and it's so large

that it won't fit on this planet. He has to create a new heaven and a new earth and a new earth, and this earth is going to be so big like 366 times larger in volume than it is now for the city of God to be able to be here. The city of God that he's planning is bigger than the continental United States.Its width or dimension is bigger than the border of Canada, the United States and the Gulf of Mexico. One side is what would be hanging up in the Gulf and then going the other way and then going up 1,500 miles. That's a huge city. Mind you, I have no way of actually being able to figure this out. But I've sort of tried to think about how many people have been born and lived on this planet to date. And, you know, maybe for the next 5, 10, 20 years too, who knows? But I'm sure that it's going to be over 100 billion,out of that amount of people, how many is God going to keep?

You know God is not a sentimental person or something. You know everything is absolutely right and wrong, and between right and wrong, true and false, and everything. There is no in-between and he is all-powerful, all-knowledgeable and we can't figure out actually how to handle that because we can't fathom it. So we may as well admit it and I think it's a good thing that God is who he is. We're very fortunate.

Anyway, that's enough of getting old. You know, it's a goal that a lot of people have, I guess, but in my case it's just a goal that a lot of people have, I guess, but in my case it's just a matter of I'm not in charge. I'll get up, have breakfast, dinner and supper, as long as it's a deal, as long as I'm supposed to, and be thankful for it. So that's all for tonight. But thank you and I wish you the best and I would ask God to bless you. Thank you.

White Skins, Tribulations : Unfolding the Story of the Israelites and the Modern Man

Chapter 4

1

2 Can you remember the last time you bought a half-ham from Walmart for $6.95? Feels like ages

3 ago, right? This stark reality of escalating living costs and its impact on our daily bread and butter,

4 especially for those clocking hours as tellers, clerks, or laborers, forms the centerpiece of our

5 conversation today. Despite the glaring challenges, we share interesting observations about

6 people's undeterred ambition to buy million-dollar homes, even in the face of potential mortgage

7 payments doubling with the advent of new interest rates.

8

9 Switching gears, we slice through the Biblical narrative, painting it as an extra-terrestrial book with

10 profound insights about the Israelites and their diaspora across the globe. Their historical journey,

11 the significance of their white skin complexion, and a speculative look into the tribulations that may

12 await them, forms the crux of this discussion. As we wrap up, we'll take a moment to ponder the

13 purpose of our daily lives, and how something as simple as hobbies can offer a sense of purpose.

14 Join us as we traverse through these engaging narratives, ending with a heartfelt wish for our

15 listeners - may you find your purpose and be blessed!

16

17

18

19 Well, good evening from Vernon, British Columbia, in the beautiful Okanagan Valley in oh in BC.

20 And it's September the 28th at about 6.40 pm and the weather's still pretty good. Hope it's good

21 where you are and hope it sticks on around for a while. I mean, like everybody would like to have a

22 nice warm fall. I'm sure of that. And so what's the big push today? Well, I think one of them is the

23 cost of living. You know, the prices go up really fast. I mean really going up.

24

25 Did I mention to you what I think I did when I went to Walmart and bought a few things. That's

26 before I moved here into the rest home and one of them was a little half-ham. You know they used

27 to be about 6.95 or something like that. Well, any Walmart had them on at $10. And I use a cart

28 there all the time. So I went in and I thought I'd get up to tell the teller no, couldn't do that, I had to

29 go into the self-serve. So I got into the self-serve and this woman came up and said you'll have to

30 get a bag. You'll need a bag. Oh, yeah, that's right. Yeah, she said you can buy one here for

31 $1.75. Ah, I said, is that right? Well, I said, it just hit me wrong. I said you know what, I can't buy

32 groceries here, I don't have a bag. So I'll tell you what, just keep your groceries and your cart and

33 we'll see you later sometime. Goodbye, and I walked out. I don't usually do things like that, but

34 anyway, I went from there. I went over to Safeway and I think most people in this country know

what Safeway is. I bought just about the same things. Cut up to the teller she's ringing things through that half ham was $16. From one store to another, $6 on a $6 ham, that's not 8%. Well, no, no. That's pretty bad, that's bad and I'm convinced that that's really hurting some people.

Some people just seem to be absolutely oblivious to this inflation and you know they seem to be in an age bracket, I don't know, 24 to 39 or something like that, and I don't hear them complaining that much. You know. I mean I don't understand how people can pay $2,400 to rent a little apartment. I mean how can they do that? Working as a teller or clerk or a laborer, how are you going to do that? That's damn near impossible. In fact, labor gets now, right now, Usually in construction or anything like that, maintenance gets $25 an hour, which works out to be four thousand a month, which is down to fifty thousand a year, which is you know what. What a guy used to think was a hell of a good wage, but you know the cost of things.

Oh man, why? I just don't know what. Is it? Because people have too much money, or a lot of money? I mean they buy million-dollar homes, eight hundred thousand, six hundred thousand, seven, eight hundred thousand and Finance it, and now they get payments of five thousand dollars a month. How do they do that? I Don't see screaming and hollering about it. I Think there's going to be. People have to let them leave their house. They won't be able to pick with the new interest rates, as there's new interest rates coming out around it. You know seven to eight percent now and they bought in maybe two and a half or three, so that's, you know, more than double their mortgage payment. When that happens, I'll bet there's quite a few that'll have to say Can't do it, sorry, goodbye. And that's sad. That's a really sad thing.

I know I've gone through that when I was younger. I Ended up in a session in 86. It was Selling condominiums built up by the hospital, nice condominiums to bedroom condos in a nice building, 17 units, 62,500. I couldn't sell, interest rates were 21%. The mortgage company that I worked with went broke, went into bankruptcy. So I just carried on for a while and just basically rented them. You know, tried to sell them and rent them and that didn't work. Finally, another company in Toronto which took over the debt of this company in Vancouver, asked me, do you want to sell my interest in Highland Park for $1? And I thought about it for a minute and I said send the paperwork Because I couldn't keep up.

I mean, even with the rent. I couldn't. I couldn't keep up with expenses and I had to settle it out somehow. I mean I had second mortgages galore on my Orchard and it was terrible. Guy across

1 the street has built a 26 unit apartment building, He lost that plus a couple of warehouses. Nobody
2 can cry on his doorstep. There was so much equity that went into oblivion, just gone. Equity gone,
3 just gone, never to get back. That's a terrible thing when things go like that, but anyway, I was a
4 lesson. I guess I Was a tough one to go through, though yeah, I go by, drive by there now in that
5 building will just still look really great. That's a good building too, but anyway, that's the history,
6
7 I can't do anything about that, but the way things are going is what bothers me. I Mean I'm at the
8 tail end of this existence that you know I'm living in, but I'm trying to get it so that it's no use for me
9 to get upset about it and save the planet and know we've got to do this and that, no, I've decided.
10 No, I can't do that, it doesn't pay for me to do that. I can't control One Iota, and neither will anyone
11 else be able to. That's going to be a big lie and people are going to suffer, I'll tell you suffer, for no
12 good reason or not. They can think it's a good reason, but it won't do any good. The governments
13 and the United Nations, whatever they'll say, we're going to save the planet if it kills you, and that's
14 what's going to happen. It's going to kill a lot of people.They don't care about it.
15
16 I came in this world in 1934 and basically I was too young to go into the army when that happened
17 and my dad was too old and so I didn't have anything to do with that and I've lived a pretty you
18 know life that you know, no big war and things like that. I've had things happen in my family that
19 were pretty bad, but other than that it's been a pretty good life for me in a way. I mean I had some
20 ups and downs, that's for sure. But I rely on one thing and I decided this maybe 15 years ago.
21 When I say 15, that means I was 75. So I think around 75 or 80, I can't remember exactly when I
22 could trust what Jesus Christ said in the Bible and I could trust what God said in the Bible and I
23 realized I couldn't really trust anyone else. But that wasn't that strong then.
24
25 It's only in the last five years that I decided I can't trust people, the human race, the media, the
26 churches, politicians, and I can't trust what my neighbor says or my daughter or my son, because
27 they've been deceived. And the big deceiver is the media. It has become the absolute enemy of
28 the people and it's done basically for money. They're paid to do this. If they don't do that, they're
29 not on the good side of the people who pay their bills. And you know, the Bible is a true book.
30 And now people say I don't know if it was inspired. I can tell you it was inspired by God. For people
31 to read it, I think it took something like 1500 years by 45 different authors. And a good example is
32 that Moses wrote the book of Genesis and that's about the creation of the world, this and that,
33 whatever I'll guarantee you that Moses was not there. Then God inspired him to write this, every
34 single word. That's why the Bible is actually an extraterrestrial book. It's not from this planet, it's

1 given to this planet, given to the people of this planet, and that's why it's been a book of books for
2 thousands of years now. It's a real handbook. The thing that people think they don't think about is
3 this one. They say oh, the Bible. Yeah, we've got a Bible, You read it, yeah, I read it.
4
5 But the main thing about the Bible is it's a book about one family, the family of Adam. Now that's
6 when you think of it, if that's an extra terrestrial book given to the earth, about one family that God
7 created and all the generations after them. That's not about families in, You know, africa, india,
8 south America, england. You know about a family I forget where he was at, but it could have been
9 Suadi Arabia or was it Israel? but he might have been in Iraq or somewhere, some part of Iraq,
10 Jordan , but anyway he was close by there. So that's where it all started. And now Israel is that
11 little sliver of land, just a sliver. You know places in Saskatchewan, I think, are bigger than Israel,
12 but it's such a thing that things all started from around there.
13
14 And you know, when the Israelites were driven out of the north part of Israel, which was the ten
15 tribes of Israel, there were six million of them. You know they had big, big families and they just
16
17 grew way faster than we grow now. And you know there's Jacob who had I don't know how many
18 wives and concubines and whatever else, and he had sons.Every one of them, until he had twelve,
19 twelve sons, and the whole story goes on and on and on about the plot, the story about Abraham
20 and the ten and twelve tribes of Israel, and goes right into the idea that when this world is finished,
21 you know, burnt to a crisp and God says he's going to create a new heaven and a new earth. So
22 this earth is going to be all different. In fact, there are those who claim for the city of God to fit on
23 this earth it has to increase in size. That's the city that's supposed to be already created in heaven
24 and will descend on this new planet. Only, that won't be the same planet. It'll be a bigger planet.
25 You know, it's so big. But that's the good news part. Until then, it's not good news. Oh yeah, I know
26 what I was going to say. The thing is, when that city descends on this planet, fifteen hundred miles
27 square, its names on the foundations are named after the apostles Israelites. The gates are
28 named for Israelites, and the twelve steps going up are all about Israelites.
29
30 Now, how important are the Israelites in the kingdom to come? It appears very important. Now, the
31 other kicker is this: who were they? Who were the Israelites? Where are they today? Are you
32 looking at one? Am I looking at one? When they were dispersed from Israel, God said they will
33 forget who they are and they'll have to travel and live for the next twenty-five, hundred and twenty
34 years before he will release the blessing that he gave to Abraham which was the blessing of land,

1 and wealth and riches, When the twenty-five, hundred and twenty years were up, bingo it
2 happened. They had moved all into Europe and basically Western Europe, mostly Scandinavian
3 countries, Ireland, Scotland, England, Belgium, Holland and they started to immigrate to North
4 America, which happened to be, it apears reserved for them. And what color skin were they?
5 You're looking at one. They were all white skinned and I believe that the source of white skinned
6 people is Israelites.
7
8 Now, the trouble that's coming is Jacob's trouble, tribulation, whatever you want to call it, and it's
9 coming and people kind of know it. You know, they can see it's going to be something that's going
10 to be bad. That's who it's going to really hit. It's the white race. They're the ones that are going to
11 suffer the very most according to that, and can't say that the white race wasn't part of the ones that
12 were given a blessing by Abraham. They got the best land on the planet. Nobody else did. They
13 got the land in Western Europe, the land in North America, the land in Australia, New Zealand,
14 South America, South Africa, and all riches come from the land. In the long run, that's where it
15 comes from. Believe me, I've seen that Alberta has some of the richest land in the world. There's
16 no question about that. On the farm we lived on when dad would break up a few acres of new land
17
18 lots of times the black dirt was at least three feet deep and fertile land, not sand and rocks. So I
19 believe that the white race has been blessed. Mind you, they were the only race that tried to
20 evangelize the world for Jesus Christ, and Missionaries went out from England all over the place,
21 the United States all over the place, Canada all over the place, nowhere else. So it was the white
22 race that tried to promote the Jesus Christ sayings and Jesus Christ book, the Bible and God's
23 book, of course.
24
25 But that's coming to an end. But then the thing that everybody forgets is time goes on. God
26 created time for us to have time morning, night, evening. Whatever That'll be finished, there'll be
27 time no more. That's what it says. This angel will come out and say time is no more, and that
28 makes it that much closer to where this world will be.
29
30 If you're a righteous enough person and chosen and righteous, you know what righteous means.
31 Righteous just means right with God. Now God wants people to be right with him. He does a lot of
32 good. He did a lot of things to try to make it that way. He got together with the Word before time
33 began and agreed beforehand that the Word would become flesh and would have to suffer and die
34 as a penalty for people breaking his law, the people that he was going to create. They would not

keep his law and his law was supreme. If they broke his law they would have to die. Now there was only one other thing, the substitute, to die, and that Jesus agreed to that. That's the Word. He agreed to that before he came to earth and became known as Jesus.

So I don't think enough people study and look into things to see what is the end game here. You know I mean when you look into it and read the promises, you know you can't beat the book of Revelation for a good book, the last book in the Bible. Whether you're a Christian or believer or whoever, you should read it Because that's the whole thing. The whole thing is right there. Jesus covers everything. There's nothing after that and it's a harbinger to what's coming and it's so great that nobody can really explain it or, you know, talk about it too much because they can't envision it. It's so great and it's going to happen. People are going to be converted, resurrected into a body that's going to live in that new life. Hmm, that's really worth talking about. You know, I mean there'll come a day when they'll say you can't talk about that on YouTube.You know that's bad, that's hate language or something that's going to get to that. I'll be banned off for even talking like this, even though I'm not a religious person. Really, I believe in God, I believe in Jesus, but I don't know if that's called religious. I think that's the only thing I can do, really, I was baptized when I was eighty, 84.

It took a while, but I got it done, I did it. Very glad I did it, because that is one thing about baptism. , no matter what age you are. It is a remission of all your sins, all your life, every one of them. You start because the idea is that you die and you are raised again with Jesus. You have no past, it's gone. That's the forgiveness part that people really need and it's not hard to do. You've got to decide that you believe what Jesus says, what God says and Knowledge that, and then there's no problem getting baptized. Just find somebody who's been baptized who can baptize you and a pool of water. It has to be immersion. The immersion is God's Signal, whatever you are dying to your sins and being raised up again. He's made it that way so it could be done. So there's things to do, things not to do.

I'm Counting and starting to count the days to December 5th, where I'm supposed to go on a cruise to the sea of Cortez. 11 days Time to look forward to that. Got a balcony unit and the only thing is I've got to figure out how to get through the airport. That's my big problem. I got to get a wheelchair. Get him to get me a wheelchair and go through. I've done this in some big airports and stated that some woman will wheel me right through Security, right through from one end to the other, right to the plane's door. Man, that's good.I Did Give her a tip.

1
2 The thing is it is really important to have something to live for, something that it's worth getting up
3 in the morning for, doesn't have to be big things. No, tomorrow I have to do this again. Yeah,
4 tomorrow I gotta go do that. Oh, yeah, that's right, I gotta do that tomorrow. That's the kind of thing
5 that gets you up in the morning.
6 Lastly, I have to kind of quit before I'm 90. I'm 90 in April, but then I don't have hobbies and I don't
7 have anyone. So this is the hobby event for like 30 years of Internet computers. I Suppose I'll carry
8 on for a while. I Want to wish you a good evening. I'd be good tomorrow and I hope I'm gonna ask
9 God to bless you, because God's blessing Really means a lot. I can't do it, but God can do it and I
10 can ask him to do that. So God bless you, I'll keep you and I'll talk to you later.
11
12
13

Embracing the Dawn of a New Jerusalem: Arlo Johnson on Christian Eschatology, Humility, and Forgiveness

Chapter 5

20 Join us on a profound journey as I, Arlo Johnson, nearing the remarkable age of 90, share the
21 transformative visions of Christian eschatology. Together we'll explore the anticipation of a new era
22 marked by Earth's dramatic renewal and the dawning of a New Jerusalem. This episode promises
23 to broaden your understanding of the biblical prophecies of Armageddon and the Millennium,
24 where Jesus Christ's pivotal role charts the course for a thousand years of peace. We'll delve into
25 the ultimate destiny of humanity and the planet—a spiritual existence within a purified world,
26 unfettered by our current earthly constraints.
27
28 As we navigate these celestial waters, we'll also reflect on the essence of humility and the power
29 of forgiveness. I'll share insights on how these virtues are key in unlocking the grace of God,
30 emphasizing that it's not through our own merit, but through Jesus's ultimate sacrifice that we find
31 the path to redemption. This discussion is an invitation to embrace the promise of spiritual

1 rejuvenation and to ponder the deeper significance of these life-transforming concepts. Concluding
2 with a moment of prayer, I encourage you to carry the message of hope and renewal from our time
3 together into your daily lives. Subscribe to our feed for more episodes that inspire and challenge
4 the soul.
5
6 It's a warm day. It's saying we're going for a heat dome of some kind, but anyway, the world
7 carries on. Big forest fires in Maui, very bad, driving them right into the ocean. Lots of bad things
8 are going on. I don't want to talk about that right now. I want you to concentrate on something else,
9 and that is what I'm going to harp about. This is the humongous future that is in front of Earth. The
10 race of people on this Earth is closing out of this age and the beginning of what I usually say is the
11 beginning of forever in a new, completely new world, in a new body, in a new everything. Okay,
12 God says I make all things new. Now here's the thing that I want to talk about and kind of discuss
13 a little. You realize this is not my idea. I have no ideas of my own. No, I want you to make sure
14 about that. The business that God has laid out, Jesus Christ basically has laid it all out and he is
15 going to build it completely, redo the Earth and redo everything. And then he says once it's done,
16 he turns it back over to his father. Now, okay, what happens is this earthly age goes by, big
17 Armageddon things, armies that blow up and from what I can see, it's going to be the big, big
18 trouble of the white race of this world. This is going to be Jacob's trouble. Anyway, the thing is that
19 God, through Jesus Christ, closes it all out, runs it for a thousand years with the help of looks to
20 me like the Israelites of this world, and then the end comes. Then the planet, he says, is going to
21 be purified by fire, bang !. It's going to be all burnt to a crisp. The whole planet will be on fire. I
22 would imagine For how long. I have no idea. He also says that in the New World there will be no
23 sea but there will be a river running out of the city of God.
24
25 Now you know, you just say it's the city of God. What the city of God is from wherever you are,
26 1500 miles straight ahead and 1500 miles maybe to the left, and then you look up 1500 miles.
27 Why? How many stories is that? Anyway, you can figure that out any way you like. That's bigger
28 than most big countries, you know. It's going to be bigger than Texas, for sure, bigger than British
29 Columbia and most likely a good half of Alberta. It's bigger than France. It's from where you are,
30 1500 miles away, that you can figure that out yourself.
31
32 That's one side, but the thing that also Is something else, Jesus Christ has all this done, the city
33 comes down, everything's done and all the Resurrected people are there in spiritual form. So they
34 all come into the city and then God descends from heaven the third heaven, way up, he descends

1 to the earth, into this holy city. Now that means that the headquarters of the universe is here and
2 you will be living in the headquarters of the universe. If you have done what Jesus Christ said.
3 Remember that Before anything happened, it was decided that he was going to die for you and me
4 Because we couldn't keep the law. And God's law is Perfect and God's law is holy and therefore
5 you can't break it and the penalty for breaking it is death. So that's what you call a real law. Either I
6 mean you don't keep the law, you're done for.
7
8 The thing that I don't know I've just heard about it. I don't know if it's really true or not, but they say
9 that God has Chosen the earth as his headquarters. You know it's not the biggest planet in the
10 universe, that's for sure. Is because of its location in the universe. That it's basically kind of sitting
11 in a window on the universe. That could be, that could be a true thing. I Mean, if you had a
12 headquarters you would want it sort of like that. At least I would think so. But anyway, all these
13 things, you know I'll be 90 in April and I'm looking forward to that. That's fine if that happens. But
14 I'm looking forward to this new city. I mean, really, you know there's nothing compared to that in
15 the whole universe. And To be able to be a citizen of that Country, universe, city, whatever, it's
16 going to be quite a thing, and you know it.
17
18 It's really hard to imagine that you could be in a form, a life form of some kind that doesn't require
19 anything. It has life in it, its spiritual life is fixed, it doesn't, I don't think it has to go to the bathroom,
20 I don't know, I doubt it and you will not need to sleep. And there's no day, there's only now, there's
21 no night there. The light is on all the time. The light comes from Jesus Christ and from God, the
22 Father. The light emanates from them. That's the permanent light. It doesn't need the Sun or the
23 moon or anything else. Yeah, you know that'll be quite a difference.
24
25 I had breakfast at quarter to seven. I'm having lunch now at quarter to twelve and I'll come back
26 quarter to five and have supper again and, if I want, there, snacks in the hub Central central
27 kitchen. You know I can see a person getting used to this.. I didn't usually eat three meals a day,
28 but what I'm saying is, Nobody can tell me that you don't have something to look forward to.
29
30 What could you have to look forward to? That is greater than that promise, and it's a promise from
31 somebody who, I believe, tells the truth about everything he said. I am the truth, the life and the
32 way. Well, I believe that. I totally believe that I didn't know what to believe for many, many years,
33 but right now, since I discovered this, I can't say that I discovered it. I mean, I kind of knew about it
34 all my life, when I was a young kid, growing up and going to Sunday school, and that I guess in the

back of my mind I kind of thought about things like that. Not that much, though. Now it's funny, as I got older, in my teens and whatever, I didn't want to, you know, I wanted to go wild, running around doing stuff. Then later on you kind of swing back into it again and you know it's pretty true.

But they say that if you bring up a child in a way that honors God and Jesus when he's young, when he's old, he will revert back to it, and so the thing is. Here's the deal in a nutshell. Here's what you should actually resvolve in your mind over and over until it gets to be real, and that is you have a future, unbelievable future. God offers it to everyone. Not everyone's going to take it because people are just plain stupid. And here's death and destruction on one hand and on the other hand, life forever in a new body, a spiritual body that will live forever and is perfect, never have anything wrong with it, and you can explore the whole universe along with God, your Father. I don't see how you can knock that and I imagine you know it's just like everything else.

It takes some work and some study and work, but the biggest thing is to be humble. If you're not humble and ask for forgiveness because nobody has been good enough to be accepted by God, God has to forgive you for everything and count on the sacrifice that Jesus made on your behalf and he will do that. And it's there and you can get it. Anyway, don't pass it by. Don't give up a gift that you could never, ever, ever replace In the meantime. I want to ask God to bless you and keep you. Thank you, goodbye.

A Journey of Gratitude and Grace at the Cusp of a Century

Chapter 6

As we sit down with the remarkable nonagenarian Arlo Johnson, his 90 years of wisdom unfold in tales that transcend time and touch upon the essence of what it means to be human. Arlo, celebrating his monumental birthday in Vernon, BC, takes us through a life rich with personal

1 triumphs, deep-rooted beliefs, and the intimate struggles that come with witnessing a world in
2 constant flux. He opens up about his gratefulness for the warmth of his community while candidly
3 discussing the challenges of reconciling his devout religious views with the evolving societal
4 attitudes towards homosexuality and gender identity, a matter close to his heart and home.
5
6 Arlo's voice, seasoned with experience, guides us through a philosophical exploration of life's
7 meaning and our spiritual destiny. Recounting a pivotal epiphany at 15 years old, he shares his
8 belief in the impermanence of material possessions against the backdrop of an eternal soul. Arlo
9 meditates on the cycle of life, the acceptance of aging gracefully, and the beauty found in the
10 rhythm of the everyday. As he bids farewell, his words leave us with a profound sense of gratitude
11 and a benediction to all who have journeyed with him through this episode—a reminder of our
12 shared trajectory towards something far greater than ourselves.
13
14
15 Well, good evening. It's Arlo Johnson from Vernon, BC. On April the 25th at 9.30 pm. Spring is
16 here. It's starting to warm up a little bit, not too much yet, but it's nice to see the spring is here, the
17 leaves are coming out and things are turning. It's nice to see the spring is here, the leaves are
18 coming out and things are turning. I was going to mention a little bit about the last few days.
19
20 April 25th, my birthday was on April 22nd. I turned 90 on Monday, April 22nd and I don't know, the
21 first day, business started like on the 21st. On Sunday, yeah, cakes and stuff and from some
22 people. On my actual birthday, I didn't really. Oh, Sunday, the day before my birthday, my sister
23 arranged for cousins and my son and his girlfriend and I guess that's about it. Four or five people
24 came over here to the Vernon Rest Home, brought a cake and cards and stuff and whatever. Well,
25 which was nice, I guess. Then, actually, on oh, I forget what day it was, but the rest home here had
26 a deal for people with birthdays and got cards and stuff there. Then I think it was on 23rd, oh, yes,
27 23rd Then went out to Desert Cove and big cake and stuff out there and people you know wishing
28 well.
29
30 I'd drive down the street and people would run out to the street waving at me and saying Happy
31 birthday. And walking through the main hall, people were waving at me. I thought, how the heck do
32 they know it was my birthday? But what it is is. I guess it's a bit of a milestone. You know, I have
33 never planned, I didn't think of myself being 90 years old and it, you know, just crept up on me. I'm
34 now yet 90 years old and out of style To the world. Well, I can't help that.

The good side, due to the fact that I've grown up with certain beliefs and, and one of them had to do with with what I was taught and all the things I went to catechism and Sunday school and church and whatever for 60 years, and what I've studied church and whatever for 60 years and what I've studied since and whatever else. One of the things that has happened in this world is that the homosexual has become more prevalent. It's been around for a long time, I don't know, throughout history, and it's a thing that is very, very, what would you say abhorrent to the creator of the universe, God and Jesus. And they are basically creators of the universe, God and Jesus, and they are basically included in the list of things that keep people out of the city of God or the book of life of Jesus Christ, along with many other things. But it was bad enough that God actually destroyed two cities and just destroyed them forever.

And then for people to say, well, it's their choice, you know. Well, of course it's their choice, but it doesn't make it right. The thing is, it seems to me so devilish that it promotes a lie. You know, gay, is it a gay lifestyle? Gay, so devilish that it promotes a lie, you know, gay lifestyle, gay, that's not what I thought gay meant when I grew up, and the gay lifestyle is couched in all kinds of love terms. And that is another lie.

People, they try to pretend to get married ,man with man and woman with woman. That doesn't work out. You see all the flashy things they do and pretend that this. This man is my wife and that just grates me. I know that that's a lie. Why, why should you promote and want to promote a lie?

And the thing that bothers me is that if people support and encourage gay lifestyles and whatever, I think they're going to be classed in the same boat as an homosexual. And God is going to say, you, don't come around me, and why would I want that to happen to somebody? That is, you know nothing worse than that can happen. You know you don't want that to happen to somebody. Now people get mad at you because you don't want it to happen. You're supposed to accept it. That's wrong. You can't accept something like that. It's not that there are not other things that are just as bad and God abhors, I know that. But why pick on one and try to glorify it? And that's what they do. They don't try to glorify people getting drunk. They don't try to glorify, you know, all kinds of things murder and robbery and killing and whatever. Well, they do in some cases, but not like that. They don't try to glorify it, not like that. They don't try to glorify it.

1 I'd say that, you take the rainbow colors and use them as your symbol. The rainbow colors were
2 given by God as a promise to the world, so that's caused problems. I've had to live with that. Now
3 I've been ostracized over that. My own family don't want to talk to me anymore because they figure
4 I'm biased and whatever. That's too bad. I hate it because I know it's wrong to do that. And the
5 thing is I didn't change. They changed, Not me.
6
7 You know you don't live 90 years and see everything that's gone on in 90 years. You know it's a
8 fair amount of time and realize that it's like in the 10, going on 90 years. You know a fair amount of
9 time and realize that in like in the last 10 years, between abortion and homosexual and gay and
10 whatever. I mean that's been the big push. Now it's transgender and this and that, all perverted
11 stuff about natural human beings and they glorify that. What it amounts to is and I've said this quite
12 a few times is it's a prediction that Isaiah made and that was who knows how long that was. That's
13 thousands of years ago, but anyway, he wrote in the book of Isaiah. It's in the book that when
14 good is evil and evil is good. You know, you are living in the last days. Well, that's exactly where
15 we are now.
16
17 Only a lot of people overlook it, plain overlook it, and say it's all just, you know modern times and
18 ha ha, ha, Oh, that's bad. That is so bad. Why in the world would a person or people willingly well,
19 I say willingly put themselves in a situation where they're going to be barred from a second
20 wonderful, perfect life forever? This life's earth cycle that we're born into actually makes us great
21 cosmic travelers. I'm going to figure out how many miles I've traveled since April 22nd 1934. And
22 I'm going to have to sit down and figure it out because I know that I'm revolving. The Earth is
23 revolving, which I'm on. We're at about, most likely, 1,000 miles per hour. It's 1,200 at the equator,
24 but we're quite a ways from the equator, so we're going a little slower on the curve. Now, that's,
25 say, 1,000 miles an hour and I'm traveling around the sun through space at 68,000 miles per hour.
26 Now, I don't know exactly how many miles it is around the sun. One year trip. I've been doing that
27 for 90 years and that makes a lot of mileage. That's what you call high mileage. Yeah, I guess,
28 instead of somebody who lives a long time, I could say that well, they're high mileage, which would
29 be true.
30
31 We are born into this world Created just like that Between a male sperm and a female egg. We're
32 created like that. A mystery of mysteries of how it all works and it all happens in an instant,
33 everything that's going to require that life to take place. Now that comes with only one thing that
34 survives, that, and that is the spirit that God puts in you when you are conceived and it leaves you

1 when you die and goes back to God who gave it to you. It most likely carries a full record of
2 everything you've ever done, and I think that's what it's there for. You are created, put together cell
3 by cell, flying together at high speed. In fact, most likely you know thousands of cells an hour
4 being produced and going here and going there, and then to end up like I am, 90 years later, still
5 going. The body is still producing stuff and looking after, healing itself and replacing itself.
6
7 Now the thing is and I knew this, I knew this and it came to me like I don't know why, but it came to
8 me like when I was 15 years old. I remember I don't know what day it was, but I remember that I
9 had this thought that came over me that what was I doing here on this planet? And I realized that I
10 was here to make a decision, and so was everyone else. I realized then that people lived and died
11 and whatever, and didn't stay here forever. So what it ends up being, is that we are given a life.
12 We didn't buy it, we didn't get it from Walmart or the hardware store. We were given a life. We
13 were given a vehicle, a body to live in. It's not ours, we didn't produce it, we didn't create i
14
15 And all of a sudden, about nine months later, we come out of this womb that the woman carries
16 and we pop open our eyes and take a look and say, oh, what is this? You know, and we see
17 people looking at us and we don't know who they are and we don't know anything. Basically or
18 maybe there might be some sort of slight instinct to know. I mean, we know that we have to suckle
19 and have food and we know what we have to eat, and if we don't eat, we'll bawl and holler and cry
20 to get it. You know things like that, survival things, but we have to learn everything and you know
21 we're kind of slow learners. It takes us a while . It takes us a year or so to even learn how to walk.
22
23 Now the thing is there's people dying. I think it's because one person dies every two seconds or
24 something like that in the world, and that's around the clock, 24 hours a day, seven days a week,
25 all the time around the clock. Now, we came into this world as a gift. We were given a body and a
26 life and we were here to make a decision about who did this for us and why. We should be
27 grateful. Some do, some don't.
28
29 Now, when we leave, we leave with the same amount as we came with Nothing. In fact, we don't
30 even have one . Our spirit has gone back to God and we're just a shell, just a wet spot on the rug.
31 But anyway, you know, that's a fact. You can't argue that, nobody can argue that. You can argue
32 and win, because that is exactly what happens to everyone we come and we leave, and the only
33 thing we are capable of doing is acknowledging that God created us and that he sent his son to
34 save us because we couldn't keep his law, and that was God's plan. In the long run, that was his

1 plan. The only way he could create sons was for someone else to take the fall for them, because
2 they couldn't quite do it. And being there, made in the image of God, and God fine-tunes the rest
3 later, because you know to cultivate somebody to be your son forever and to think like you and do
4 like you and have the mind of God and whatever, hopefully.
5
6 Now, I think the worst possible thing is that people want to believe that there's nothing and they do
7 it in full realization that there's no hope for them, none, zero. And I think about that so much. I think
8 that how, what a total waste for a person to live on this planet for 50 to 100 years or whatever it is,
9 and fail, just plain fail, fail to do one simple thing that God wanted acknowledgement, that he had
10 made arrangements to save you. Now, human beings are in such a class that we're most likely
11 rated way higher than we realized by God Almighty. It's because he created us in his own image
12 and from a little bit of bits and pieces here and there, it appears to me that the angels in heaven
13 and spiritual beings are basically not jealous but in awe of human beings, because they are a
14 spark of the eternal God. They are created in the image and everything of God. Nobody else is
15 created in the image of God.
16
17 That God created and to arrange a universe in such a way that was compatible for life on earth, for
18 his children, and to change the universe around afterwards to create an eternal kingdom where his
19 children would reside with him. Which means he said he's going to create a new heaven and a
20 new earth. New heavens that's a lot to change and a new earth. This earth is going to be dissolved
21 and redone and it's I mentioned this before the city of God that God is creating, or Jesus is
22 creating. Jesus said I'm going to prepare a place for you. So it's obvious he's the builder, and it's
23 so large that it won't fit on this planet. He has to create a new heaven and a new earth, and this
24 earth is going to be so big, like 366 times larger in volume than it is now for his city of God to be
25 able to be here. The city of God that he's planning is bigger than the continental United States. Its
26 width or dimension is bigger than from the border of Canada, and the Gulf of Mexico. One side it
27 would be hanging out in the Gulf and then going the other way and then going up 1,500 miles.
28 That's a huge city.
29
30 Mind you, I have no way of actually being able to figure this out, but I've sort of tried to think about
31 how many people have been born and lived on this planet to date, and, you know, maybe for the
32 next 5, 10, 20 years too, who knows? But I'm sure that it's going to be over 100 billion, So out of
33 that amount of people, how many is God going to keep? And it's not going to be everyone, God is
34 not a sentimental person or something. You know everything is absolutely right and wrong,

1 between right and wrong, true and false, and everything. There is no in-between, and he is all-
2 powerful, all-knowledgeable, and we can't figure out actually how to handle that, because we can't
3 fathom it. So we may as well admit it, and I think it's a good thing that God is who he is. We're very
4 fortunate.
5
6 Anyway, that's enough of getting old. You know, it's a goal that a lot of people have, I guess, but in
7 my case it's a goal that a lot of people have, I guess, but in my case it's just a matter of I'm not in
8 charge. I'll get up, have breakfast, dinner and supper, as long as it's a good deal, as long as I'm
9 supposed to, and be thankful for it. So that's all for tonight. I thank you and I wish you the best and
10 I would ask God to bless you. Thank you.
11
12

Contemplating the Sacred and the Secular in Life's Grand Tapestry

Chapter 7

18 As winter's chill thaws into the promise of spring, our latest episode finds me musing on the
19 curious dance between eternal divine commandments and the mutable laws of humankind. With
20 Vernon, British Columbia's gentle winter as my backdrop, I explore the natural cycles that govern
21 our lives and question the peculiar construction of our modern calendar. Why does it not sync with
22 the celestial clockwork God has set in motion? The discussion unfolds to contrast the immutable
23 nature of divine law with the ever-shifting landscape of human legislation, where laws are as
24 transient as the political winds that shape them. I probe the sacred tenets of the Ten
25 Commandments, critiquing the liberties taken by religious institutions in their interpretation, and
26 reflect on the grand design God has for our existence, stretching beyond the simple act of
27 procreation to the spiritual sons and daughters in His kingdom.
28
29 In a world where every moment is chronicled by a divine ledger, I share a profound personal
30 experience that underscores the interconnectedness of our lives with the celestial narrative. My
31 story—a revelation about the conception of my first son—serves as a testament to the belief that

1 our lives unfold according to a preordained path within God's vast plan. As we tread through these
2 spiritually charged discussions, we also delve into the significance of faith and hope, holding fast to
3 the truths personified by Jesus Christ. I leave you with a message of spiritual tenacity, encouraging
4 listeners to anchor themselves in the principles that elevate us above the terrestrial fray, and I
5 extend a heartfelt blessing, hoping that our words may inspire reflection and bring a touch of grace
6 to your journey.
7
8 Good evening. It's 8.15 pm in Vernon, British Columbia, where I'm speaking from, and it'll let me
9 take just a quick look here. Yeah, it's about right around freezing right now in Vernon, British
10 Columbia, and, you know, not too bad. I mean, we're just about at the half point of February and it
11 looks like it's going to be about like this right through the end of the month. If that's the case, we
12 really had a pretty easy winter. I don't know what it's like we are at, but the thing I look forward to
13 and I tell you I really do as I get older, I look forward to more and more and I just sort of watch,
14 watch it, and it's like I don't know a big deal for me.
15
16 Spring is coming, the start of a new year, you realize that. You know our day starts at midnight.
17 What a stupid thing. Our year starts on January the 1st in Canada, you know that's like saying it
18 starts on January 1st at 12 midnight in the snow bank in Saskatchewan, at 20 below. That's when
19 our year starts. What a dumb thing. Nothing we can do about it. You realize that God's calendar is
20 totally different. This would have been a new day. It would have started at around I don't know
21 6:00 pm. God says the day ends at sundown and a new day starts. Now can you argue with that?
22 That's exactly what happens, not at midnight. And then he says a new year starts around the 10th
23 or 11th of April in the month I think they call it Abebe. Now that to me would be also very
24 reasonable. A new year starts, winter is over, the green grass starts and there's the rebirth of
25 another year. The sun goes down. That's the end of that day. There's no more day left. You start a
26 new day and it's dark and it goes over and the sun comes up again in about 10 hours.
27
28 You know, it makes me really wonder that the human race thinks it can make laws. It really does. I
29 watched the Congress of the United States going out and talking on this and that the one side was
30 just ragging against the other side. Democrats have got one guy that just keeps on and the other
31 side rags right back and the next day they do it again. Now what kind of good does that do? Do
32 they think that if they do that, people think they're doing a good job and will reelect them? Mistake
33 they're making is that they allow them to be there too long. You know, every time they make a law,

very few times they make laws that are a good law. It might be good for one group or something, but not for everybody. It's not a level law. Then they sort of water it down and change it over years.

You know, when God said that if you eat a garden of the tree of the good and evil or you know that you will die, well that's what happens we're all sentenced to death. We're all that are sentenced to death on account of that. And it's simple. His law is absolute. There's no getting around it. His law is so absolute that he had to allow his son to die in our place because his law demanded it and his is a holy law, the law that would run the universe and everything else. He can't change his own law just because something comes up and you know that's really tough. It can't be a tougher penalty than that. If you break this law, you're dead, you're gone, you die, you won't be around. That's a tough penalty. There's no tougher penalty than that. So when God makes laws, the only thing if people would think about it and that you know, like really think about it is that all his laws are for your and my benefit. The first four laws I believe are four or five is to worship God and to follow his laws. The other six are how you treat each other, how we treat each other in things, and that's the ten laws. Now you have groups of people, even you know I mean you get admitted because it's an actual fact.

The Catholic Church rewrites, rewrote the text, commandments, eliminated one and added one, They write their own Bible to suit them. I wonder how that's going to turn out. I don't think so. I have to wonder, or you have to wonder. You know what's going to happen. Somebody's going to pay for that. God is not going to allow that.

In certain things he said that anyone who takes away what is in the book of revelation? He says if anyone takes away from this book of revelation, that you know he will take away from them the book of life and if anyone adds to it, he will add the plagues of life to it. So making laws and saying we ought to handle the law, well, that's great to say that, but you know we're not capable of really making laws. We're supposed to follow the law. We're supposed to follow a set of principles that the Creator of the universe has put down. And you know, the thing is he knew that we weren't going to be able to do that. He knew that when he created us and he gave us warnings and all that sort of stuff, but he still took the chance and created us with the idea that many of us would follow his plan and he would be able to have sons.

Now he didn't say sons and daughters, he said sons. And the reason for that is that the business of procreation and all that will be over and there's no way he would want two sexes living forever in

1 his kingdom, because look at the problem on earth with it Fighting, it's not all that time the womb is
2 not required anymore. So his plan is for sons. He has many sons. Now, if you think about God and
3 his production of the universe, of things in the universe, when he makes flowers on a field, how
4 many does he make? His power is just unlimited practically, and he does other things. That's
5 unlimited practically. The stars you can't count the stars and yet he claims he calls them by name.
6 Now the thing is, you know, that's quite a thing, the idea that you know he would do this to have
7 sons.
8
9 He wanted sons and Adam was his first son, so he called him the son of God, and so that means
10 we're in the form of Adam. Adam wasn't just created, he was formed and set. He formed Adam out
11 of the dust of the ground and blew in his nostrils the breath of life. He was formed. I'm sure that
12 you and I are the same form, totally as Adam. Now you know, if you're a woman listening to this,
13 you say what are you talking about? That's exactly what I'm talking about, whether people like it or
14 not.
15
16 But here's the thing: a woman has just as much chance, or whatever, as being in the kingdom of
17 God as a man has. The only thing is she won't be a woman. She will be the same as the man,
18 being there as a son of God, and I can't see anything wrong with that. Why would anybody
19 complain about that? When woman was created, to be a help to man and carry the womb and
20 reproduce. Now, let's face it, a woman has reproduced a lot. Well, this world would be populated
21 with eight billion people. It is all done automatically. God has such a system, a place, that we don't
22 even realize it's so automatic, on autopilot. I mean, God doesn't come along and say you got to
23 create another child tonight at 8 o'clock at night or 9 o'clock. He puts in an urge into the men that
24 basically add into the women. But basically I think it's a stronger urge in men and they want to
25 plant the seed and the better looking the woman is, the more they want to plant the seed. Now
26 they don't have anything to do with it except the little muscular mechanics they go through. It's all
27 automatic. They carry the seed, they realize they have 10,000 sperm in them, most likely a lot
28 more. But on these sperm each one could create another human being. Many are spilled and gone
29 and whatever Many go in at a time.
30
31 I would imagine there's a whole bunch of sperm that goes in in one ejaculation and only one gets
32 into the egg. It has to hit it just right to cut, make its various head in there and leave the information
33 it carries for the next human being, because the egg is the feeding area that will feed the sperm
34 and create cells and there's enough in that egg that the woman has that most likely does a whole

1 bunch, most likely lasts for quite a while, Because it has to last until the child, and can form blood
2 vessels and whatever else. Otherwise it wouldn't be able to. But when I'm getting at it, it's all done
3 automatically. The woman doesn't decide to build blood vessels, she doesn't decide how he's
4 going to be fed or whatever else. The man doesn't do anything except plant the seed. He's never
5 seen the seed, he doesn't know what it is, but he has it.
6
7 Now you talk about an automatic system to create all kinds of humans that God loves. You know,
8 the thing is that there is something in the humans that God puts in at the moment of conception
9 and that is the human spirit he receives. That's the automatic thing that happens. That spirit stays
10 with the person all his life and I believe that spirit is connected to some kind of system that records
11 every breath that the person takes, every thought. Everything is recorded somehow, and when you
12 die and you outlive your life, that returns to who put it there. It's like it's back to God and it's like just
13 come back and talk it away, or the resurrection, when it'll be called up again.
14
15 Now, I didn't come up with that plan, did you? No, we didn't have anything to do with it at all. And
16 you know, it's funny how some things work. I remember when we were on a trip to Saskatchewan
17 one time it was in the fall , and we didn't have the kids with us my wife and I just took off to
18 Saskatchewan to visit a guy that used to work with me and anyway we were upstairs in their
19 upstairs bedroom where we were staying there overnight and my wife and I we basically had sex.
20 But that's the only time, only time, that it hit me and it was like as soon as that act was over I just
21 kind of stopped and I said, oh, I didn't know it was going to be a son, but I knew at that moment
22 that she was going to be pregnant, I knew that whatever had been done right there, and it just
23 happened like two minutes afterwards, five minutes afterwards maybe, and it was like you know,
24 when I'm trying to explain this and I think you may be known this there are times when something
25 happens to you that it makes you stop and you wonder what happened? Is that what happened?
26 What happened? And I realized I knew that there was going to be a child right there. I didn't know
27 what happened to my son and why that was. I don't know why. I really don't know. That too was
28 my first son and then we had another son.
29
30 But there's strange things that happen to everybody's life and I think a lot of it is. You know how
31 sensitive we are to it. If we're not sensitive to it, it'll go by right over. Who knows? But there are
32 other times when it appears to be something, just like a spirit or a thought or something comes
33 over you and you know it. It's different, it's not the same. It stops you and you're cracked
34 practically, and that's something to kind of watch for, because things like that happen, like

1 I believe that if you pray and talk to God, the Creator of the universe, which you're entitled to do
2 under the auspices of Jesus Christ, that's how you got to do it. You got to say I'm praying to you
3 and your son's name, Jesus Christ. That's how I come to you. That's the calling card that he has to
4 have Now. That's open right now. It's open tomorrow. It's open tonight. It's open the next day. It's
5 open 24 hours a day. There's no charge, and it's instant. It works instantly.
6
7 God knows when you pray. He knows when anybody in the whole world prays. He can hear the
8 world pray all at once. He can hear them all at once when I say God is great, they have to
9 remember how they got to write the word great. It's so great that it's a fathomable test. And the
10 thing is, the wonderful thing is that if a person ends up being in the book of Jesus Christ's book of
11 life, which is the important thing that he'll know about these things, that'll be knowledge that a
12 person will receive and I'm sure it's going to just blow people away because they have ever dreamt
13 of this stuff, kind of things. And you have to remember something that's going to keep you going
14 for eternity.
15
16 That means forever. Yeah, that's a long time, but imagine there are such depths of things that will
17 happen that you'll be totally, totally immersed in it and you never sleep. You never have to do
18 anything. You have life in you, total. You don't have to eat, you don't have to sleep, you don't sleep
19 as there's no night and you don't sleep anyway. You're, you're, you're awake, and I wonder if you
20 know you're on, just like on duty, 24 hours a day, and then say 24 hours a day, there's no day
21 there. There is no day, it's just time. But there is no time anymore. It's God's time, which is now
22 forever. There's no midnight and morning and afternoon, none of that.
23
24 When you caught it, caught a play. When you do start to think about stuff like this and you caught
25 it, played it it blows your mind away, I'll tell you. It makes you think that you know a person really
26 should be doing better, trying to be doing the things that God requires. Well, anyway, we've gone
27 over a few minutes here. That's good enough, and I hope that the world's news is not getting you
28 down. Don't let it get you down. Doesn't matter. It's planned, it's gonna happen. Every single thing
29 that happens is all planned. I'm convinced of that. Totally planned, every single thing, and it'll
30 progress along. Some of it will be hated and some of it will be glad to see, but there will be a lot of
31 things we won't like to see. A moment may have to suffer for it too, but anyway, I don't think it's
32 gonna be too dull. You know, I think it's a pretty exciting time coming up.
33

Regardless of what happens, it's the result, the end comes. That's what hope is and what you can believe. Your hope is and you can believe because God is the truth and Jesus Christ is the truth. So I am the truth, the way in life only comes to the father through me, well, I don't think it hurts to mention that every so often, because you know we're like sheep. We go astray pretty easy and hard to keep us on track, that's for sure. Anyway, that's very good for today and I would appreciate it if you stayed this long. You're, you're a good guy if you did that, a good girl if you did that. But thank you very much for that and I would also like to say God bless you and I hope he does. Thank you very much and good night.

Spring Awakening: Navigating God's Timeless Plan and Our Spiritual Journey Through Life and Beyond

Chapter 8

As the buds of Vernon, British Columbia burst into life, I, Arlo Johnson, invite you to join me in a soul-stirring odyssey that melds the freshness of spring with the profound mysteries of time and God's cosmic blueprint. In a symphony of reflection, we traverse God's meticulously planned calendar, from the biblical Abib to the grand tapestry woven with each moment of our existence. With the blooming flowers as our backdrop, we embark on a journey to understand the insignificance of worldly endeavors in the face of securing our names in God's book of life, and the breathtaking vista of a new heaven and earth that awaits.

Venturing further into the spiritual realm, I share my intimate walk with faith in the Lutheran church, scrutinizing the depths of religious teachings that often leave the eschatological puzzles incomplete. We grapple with the contentious practices of the Catholic Church and open up about the hierarchy within God's Kingdom, questioning our eternal roles and the transformative power of belief in Jesus Christ. As the chapter of life inevitably closes, I contemplate the urgency of seizing the day, leaving a legacy that echoes through eternity and sparks inspiration long after our final

1 breath. Join me in this episode as we navigate these topics with sincerity and a longing for divine
2 wisdom.
3
4
5 Good morning. It's Arlo Johnson in Vernon, British Columbia, coming to you at 10.15 am on March
6 the 16th, and hopefully it's about spring. It'll be up to about 60 degrees Fahrenheit this afternoon,
7 which is not bad, but it is the 16th of March, so it should be expected. So the goodness of spring,
8 which I've said before, if you've listened to my podcast, is something that I actually really look
9 forward to and I think every mind, not just me, I mean everyone actually looks forward to spring.
10 When you see the activity that goes on around the different sites, you know the well I know what
11 you call them gardening sites and whatever there's people just running around packing bags of
12 this and bags of that, pots and all kinds of stuff every spring.
13
14 I think I mentioned this before and I'm going to mention it again the difference between what
15 mankind thinks is the right way to learn things and God thinks the right way to learn things, and I
16 think in all cases God is superior and God is right. For instance, spring in God's world starts
17 around the 12th of this calendar called Abib, which I believe is around April in this calendar, so
18 around the 12th of April, and it certainly starts out here and he said that's, but that's spring. But it's
19 not just spring. That is the new year. The winter is over and now a new year and it's not like we do
20 with January, the 1st at midnight in a snowbank somewhere on the highway in Saskatchewan. I
21 mean, I can't follow that at all. God's day starts at sunset, the old day ends at sunset and a new
22 day begins at sunset. Now there's also 30 days of the month every month, and the adjustment is
23 made once every four years. Somehow I forget how it's done. But now, when you think about the
24 way God's mind must work, or plan that works, and the way we do things where we're utterly, you
25 know, we're inferior by far. God does things that are very common sense, and I mean let's place it
26 as a race of people. We don't practice very much common sense. There's some people who do, I
27 guess, but the majority do not. So I guess that's the life we have. Someday, I guess, we'll go by
28 God's plan, God's rules.
29
30 It's very interesting, when you study this a little bit, that God has a plan and it's a plan and we are
31 part of that plan and we're in that plan Every day we get up. We're part of that plan and it's another
32 slice of time in that plan. The plan is, you know, it's not changeable, it's absolutely built into stone.
33 Basically, you know, how long do you think in our time? Say, do you think God took the form that
34 this plan was in this age on the earth and the different earth ages and now this earth age? It's like

God was trying a few scenarios and he settled on this one and for some reason or other I certainly can't prove it or anything like that but it appears to me it's like we're in the final run of this plan. It's like this plan has been kind of run through once before and now we're in the final plan and that means that I am here printing a book having you happen to read it, it means that that was part of the plan. That is how precise the plan is.

It has to be like that, because all of nature is built on a reducing scale. You know, like all the animals and all this stuff, they last for only so long. They're not permanent. And there's now, I think, thousands of species of animals that are gone. There's been species of humans too. But when God comes along and says or Jesus says I'm going to build a place, I'm going to prepare a place for you so that you can be with me.

Well, that puts things in a different light altogether. That means we've settled on a plan and God wants sons, he wants a big family and, let's face it, if we could grasp the level of magnitude that God deals with like he doesn't, he never exaggerates, never. He never embellishes anything. Every word he says is a powerful word. It's necessary to what he is saying and being that God is Almighty, you know, and he is a great spirit who can change or do anything, is most likely in the position where he deserves and what requires, the top, largest presence in the whole universe, because he, the universe, belongs to him, everything.

Now, if that's the case, the city of God which we know the size of is 1500 miles square, 1500 miles high, we can't visualize it. You can't remember how many floors or what it would be, 1500 miles up high, but what would be there? And basically, I certainly didn't know until just lately that the city wouldn't fit on this planet. I've never said anything about that. He just said I will create a new heaven and a new earth, and which means he's going to have an earth that is going to accommodate the size of the city. And to do that, from what I understand and what I've read these people have done calculations on it says that the world, this world's size, has to increase by 366 times. So instead of an 8,000 diameter world, 8,000 miles, 4,000 radius, but 8,000 diameter, it's going to have to be tons and tons bigger than that. But I guess the only way you can explain that is because this is where God is going to be. This is going to be his headquarters and we're going to live in his headquarters.

If we are in his book of life, that's the most important thing. All this other stuff and we have elections and we have this and we have that and we fight about this and argue about that None of

1 that is really that important. I mean, it's kind of day-to-day important on a small scale, but what's
2 really important is that if we are going to be in Christ's book of life, that is the thing I mean. You tell
3 me if there's something more important for you or me. I'd like to hear it. But I know there isn't and
4 I'm sure you know there isn't, and it depends on how much procrastination. We do or had, and I
5 certainly know about that too, and I think it makes it really tough.
6
7 If you get to a point in your life where you actually believe what Jesus Christ has said and what's
8 going to happen. He says this will happen and that will happen. You believe that, you finally
9 believe it. And then you sit back and look at the world around you and you are Just about blow
10 your way when you see people who don't even know about it, think about it or do anything about
11 that or even take it seriously and make you wonder. You know, I mean, I can't get anyone to do it, I
12 Can't say you do this and you do that, and then you know you'll be in this kingdom. No, only God
13 can do that. He's the only one that can call people to Christ, his son, who is going to be the judge
14 of the world and who is going to be, who is the savior of the world and who is also God. The father,
15 the son and the Holy Spirit make up God. Yeah, I don't know if it ever bothers you or makes you
16 wonder. When you look at somebody, do you actually Say to yourself man, are they going to be in
17 God's kingdom or not? The thing is I, you know, I personally totally believe what God says. I totally
18 believe what Jesus Christ has said. It took me a long time to do that, but Once I did that, that was
19 a big
20 relief for me, because I could believe everything that Jesus Christ said and it cleared up a lot of
21 things, a lot of things.
22
23 I went to the Lutheran church for about 60 years, on and off, not the stretches I'd, you know, you
24 know, go very often, but All during that time I never even heard about the book of Revelation. I
25 Never even heard about these different things. I said right in the Bible. I mean why did I take
26 catechism? I was confirmed in the Lutheran church. Never Heard about it, told about. It Was
27 always these fluff things sort of like Traditionals, traditions, you do this, you do that and and you
28 know I, that's not nobody bad in the kind of Lutheran church or anything like that. They're all good,
29 I don't think they're good for people. I'm good for people Because they are like milk toast. They're
30 weak and they don't seem to Form up or have a stance on things. That's not good.
31
32 When I read about the Catholic Church, I just think to myself. You know, the largest church, the
33 largest Christian church anyway, on the planet, and it is when you read what they are and what
34 they've done and what they believe and what they've changed. And they said not to change things,

1 and they say, oh yeah, we can change. You know, to me they're just a preview of the Antichrist
2 Church, which I think they're going to be False prophet or whatever it's called. I can see that. Their
3 whole deal. You know, taking the place of you know they say that they are the priests who can
4 forgive sins and all that sort of stuff. No, I don't think you can. The Pope is infallible now.
5
6 But all these things are lies, you know, and they are basically lies. And we're living in a lying, lying
7 world. You can't go, for a day with other people or somebody lying to you and I mean they do it
8 honestly, they don't think they're lying. They spread lies and deception because they don't know
9 any better. That's all they know, that's what they've been told, that's what they saw on the news,
10 and they cannot separate the facts that the news is not. It's not trustworthy. You can't believe the
11 news anymore. It is so slanted.
12
13 And so the whole deal is basically the description of Satan, who takes the truth and then puts a lie
14 in it. He twisted it. That's how he sells the lie, and I think it's a good thing that he's been judged,
15 which he has. Satan has been judged already and he's waiting for his first go in the hole for a
16 thousand years. And you know, you can see why God is going to let him out because he's going to
17 gather up all the people who still are against God, against everything. There'll still be people like
18 that. He's going to gather them all up and then that's going to be the wiping that's going to clean
19 again. Yes, it's a plan. There's no doubt about that. One of the mysteries really is who is going to
20 be in the kingdom of God forever. You know, Jesus said there are those who will be the greatest in
21 the kingdom and those who will be the least.
22
23 When I read that and thought about that for a while, I thought you know, that opens up a whole big
24 thing. There's a hierarchy there of some kind. Then there's the big city, huge, huge city, and the
25 earth way bigger than it is now. Is there some way that the audience is going to make a situation
26 where people will have to work their way out of something on outside the city, it's said, because
27 outside the city are dogs and this, and that you know that's what it says. I'm not saying that, that's
28 what it says. And yet the gates of the city are never closed, day or night. There is no day or night.
29 There's only day, only daytime. There is no night, there is no time.
30
31 When people say that you live forever, well, I guess that's one way of saying it, but it is that you
32 live where there's no time, there is no time, and you have an indestructible spiritual body that you
33 live in. It's not physical, there's no blood veins, you don't go to the toilet, I don't think. And they still
34 have. They have meat, they eat, I guess, or have banquets or something. I mean it's hard to figure

1 out, isn't it? Well, I don't know if that's how it happens. I don't know if they say it's about banquets,
2 but Ah, yeah, well, it could be some kind of that's a very important saying hey, so if you're like I
3 am, if you're thinking that there may be a chance, that if you ask for forgiveness and believe in
4 Jesus Christ and believe in God, that there may be a chance that you may see the time when God
5 will say to you go to the right and enjoy the things that God has provided for you, and hopefully not
6 say, go to the left. I don't know you. That's well, that's going to be it.
7
8 And once a person dies, you can't actually do much about it anymore. He only can do something
9 as long as he is physically and mentally alive. Once he dies, that is the end of his life. That's the
10 section. So you know, a person who doesn't want to really procrastinate forever can't guarantee it.
11 Anyway, good thing that there's a way to do this. Only it's hopefully we have to do it and this
12 hopefully, hopefully somebody will pay attention to that, I don't know. Anyway, thank you for
13 listening and God bless you and we'll see you later.
14
15

Confronting the Abortion Debate: A Reflection on Faith, Moral Landscapes, and National Identity
18
19

Chapter 9
21 A vivid dream in the dead of night set the stage for my revelation on the abortion debate—a
22 revelation that I can't keep to myself. As I stand on the precipice of my 90th birthday, the memories
23 of a different Canada, one from my youth, flood back, and I feel compelled to share my thoughts
24 on how abortion has reshaped our nation's moral and cultural landscape.
25
26 This episode isn't for the faint of heart, as I confront the uncomfortable truth that each abortion, in
27 my view, extinguishes a potential life that's divinely sparked at the moment of conception. With
28 religious observances setting the scene, I challenge the defense of abortion as women's
29 healthcare and scrutinize the demographic changes within our country, pondering the long-term
30 consequences on the white race and the Christian faith. There's a chilling effect, a sense that
31 we're at a crossroads, and I urge listeners to consider the spiritual and national repercussions of a
32 practice I believe goes against God's will.

1
2 Join me for a good afternoon, good morning, 10.30 am in Vernon, British Columbia. Hope you're
3 all doing fine. I guess today's the Sabbath day. Yesterday was Good Friday and tomorrow is
4 Easter Sunday, so I would imagine people are celebrating that in different ways. But anyway,
5 putting that aside today I'm not going to talk about that too much today. I wanted to mention to you
6 today that I woke up in the middle of the night last night dreaming about a situation. I woke up
7 really angry, cranky, and it was all about abortion and I was going through all these scenarios and
8 stuff. And I was going through all these scenarios and stuff and it made me realize how important
9 this abortion business really is to this world and especially to this country. It's destroying it.
10
11 People, I think, have been brainwashed into the idea that it's, you know, a woman's right to do this
12 to kill babies . Just call them a fetus instead of a baby, and men who go along with it and
13 encourage it and whatever, pay for it if they have to. And then you have people like Planned
14 Parenthood who call it ? Health care, women's health care. You know that's devilish right there,
15 because that is such a lie. But the problem really is? It really is murder and killing. There's no
16 doubt about that, Because I'm convinced that when a woman gets pregnant, the man's sperm, the
17 one that finally makes it into the egg, fertilizes it right there and right there is the spark that starts
18 life, and immediately after that, God gives it a human spirit. That happens most likely all at once.
19 Now to say that you can get rid of that, it's my body and I can do what I want with it, that's a big lie.
20 And then to say that it doesn't matter, that it's not a human or anything else, that's a big lie. It's just
21 as human as you or I am Instantly. Now, what that does to a country, you know for the fact, that
22 when you kill a Canadian and then bring in a stranger from a foreign land ,your Country is
23 destroyed..
24
25 This is against God's will for this world and for his people and for his family and for his children.
26 Now I can't see how they're going to get away with this at all. And men won't get away with it. Men
27 could be even more responsible than the woman, because he carries the seed, he plants the seed
28 in the woman and then he says, oh, go ahead and kill it, we don't need it. Or she says, I want to kill
29 it, I'm not going to have it. Or the middle-aged wife says I'm not going to have this interrupting me
30 and the 30-year-old woman working in the office as you know, she's getting to be a manager or
31 whatever oh, I can't have this to disrupt my life.
32
33 And then the other ones who say we, I have a right to have sex free of consequences, just like a
34 man, and that's what they demand. And the public gets bamboozled into that. And the next thing,

you know, all the politicians agree with that and they destroy their country. They absolutely destroy the country. They kill their own children and bring in strangers and they say, oh, that's fine, it's not fine. In God's eyes it's not fine.

And anybody who agrees with God's way of this ,it's not fine. Absolutely, will create the wrath of God. There is no way around that. God allows it as a curse to a nation that does this. They destroy themselves. And he allows it Because every single one, every single child that's aborted, is already one of God's children. He says don't worry about who can kill the body, Worry about who can kill your soul or your spirit, and they can't kill their spirit. So the ones who do abortion, promote abortion, will be held accountable. And I believe that, and you know, it's not that I have anything to do with making laws or anything, but it's just I understand why God hates this and hates it with a passion that says there will be consequences. God's wrath will be the end winner on this, there's no doubt about that.

Those who support abortion, mass abortion, like they do now, are going to be guilty in God's eyes. That's for sure. And if that's their choice, then that's their choice. But I wouldn't want to be in their shoes because, How are they going to answer when Christ says what are you doing about killing children? What is your explanation for killing children? What is your explanation for that? They're going to have to Remember God says you live so many years and then you die, and then you face the judgment. And that is the judgment, and you will be judged. I will be judged. Every single one will be judged.

I believe that there is no way in this world that abortion will be abolished or anything like that, Because the evilness of people, women's tendency to go along with Satan's biggest faults, which is jealousy and vanity, will continue on a great scale and most likely more, and God will allow it. He will say fine, if you want to do that, you're digging your own grave, condemning yourself. So me saying that you know I hate abortion and God hates abortion and a lot of other people do too is going to solve the problem. No, it's gone too far for that. People would rather risk their future life totally due to the fact that they will accept and promote abortion. You don't have to have an abortion to be in God's crosshairs. You know, If you promote and you agree with abortion, you're in God's crosshairs. You're not going to get away with that.You're promoting the death of God's children. They're not your children.

I wish people would have the dream like I did last night about it. That might change their mind. But I suppose that's not going to happen either. So you know people will say, well, you're very

1 pessimistic . Maybe. I don't know if you take it as being pessimistic. I take it as being factual. And
2 it's a fact that people are killing their children and it's false. It's a dirty lie, it's a satanic deal.
3
4 They don't believe these people who do this wouldn't dare do that because they know that would
5 be wrong. Anyway, Christ said to remember him to break bread, drink wine. This is my body, he
6 said. Drink wine. He said this is my blood I've given to you. And if they did that they'd think twice. I
7 know that it's rare.
8
9 Now that you know, people go and have communion. I believe that a person should be celebrating
10 the Passover and not Easter. Easter is a devilish thing, I mean what? Well, sun worshippers, one
11 thing, and fashion hats and whatever else and bunnies and eggs and kids dancing around chasing
12 bunnies and egg hunts and this and that, and what could be farther from the fact that Christ hung
13 on a cross and died for you? Is that how you celebrate? That Is death like that. That's a bad thing.
14 That's Easter. Passover is Passover. Passover is when God passed over the people of Israel and
15 said put your blood around your door and I will pass over you around your door and I will pass over
16 you. And Christ had a Passover meal with his disciples the night before he was crucified and he
17 told them that that's a big difference Life is.
18
19 You know, life is pretty serious. There's no question about that, Especially when you understand
20 what's at stake. You're born into this world, you come into this world, You wake up and all of a
21 sudden you're here. You don't know how you got here, you don't have a clue. You're there, You're
22 opening your eyes and you're looking at these people and whatever's going on here. Pretty soon
23 you learn to talk and walk and whatever. You die and you leave with nothing.
24
25 So, in other words, you go through this business of life, which I knew when I was 15 years old, that
26 the only reason you're here is to make a decision yes or no. Do you believe that God sent Jesus
27 into this world to save the world, yes or no? That's the criteria If you're going to go into the next
28 step, which is going to be a totally different world and that does not have an end. This one is, you
29 know, a transparent deal, but it has an end, that's the right word. But anyway, it's all been done.
30 We're in the plan and that's the plan going on and you can bet your bottom dollar that God knows
31 exactly how it's going and when it's going, what you're going to be doing and not doing. What your
32 neighbor's going to do, you maybe don't know, but he knows, and I could tell you that it is if you
33 once understand what happens to you after this life is over. You're right, life is over. That's a big

1 relief Because you're not in charge of it, but you can be told what will happen to you and basically
2 read the book of Revelation. It helps a lot, A lot.
3
4   went to the Lutheran church for 60 years.
5 they never even talked about the book of Revelation, Not once. How do you like that? Well, I found
6 out. I didn't like that. Now I'm going to say one last thing about abortion. It's devilish. If you believe
7 in it, you are wrong. There is nothing more wrong than that. I hope you don't think that that's a
8 good thing to do, that you're sucked in by a lie, because it's a huge lie, and that you can break
9 away from that and realize that in God's eyes, you are very, very important. You are so important
10 that he was willing to, you know, do anything to save you, and he did. With that, I would say have
11 a happy Passover. That's what I would say. Forget this stupid Easter bunny business. Anyway, I
12 promise not to be this pessimistic and hard next time. Thank you for listening and God bless you.
13
14

15 # Spring Awakening: Navigating God's Timeless Plan and
16 # Our Spiritual Journey Through Life and Beyond
17
18 ## Chapter 10
19
20 As the buds of Vernon, British Columbia burst into life, I, Arlo Johnson, invite you to join me in a
21 soul-stirring odyssey that melds the freshness of spring with the profound mysteries of time and
22 God's cosmic blueprint. In a symphony of reflection, we traverse God's meticulously planned
23 calendar, from the biblical Abib to the grand tapestry woven with each moment of our existence.
24 With the blooming flowers as our backdrop, we embark on a journey to understand the
25 insignificance of worldly endeavors in the face of securing our names in God's book of life, and the
26 breathtaking vista of a new heaven and earth that awaits.
27
28 Venturing further into the spiritual realm, I share my intimate walk with faith in the Lutheran church,
29 scrutinizing the depths of religious teachings that often leave the eschatological puzzles
30 incomplete. We grapple with the contentious practices of the Catholic Church and open up about
31 the hierarchy within God's Kingdom, questioning our eternal roles and the transformative power of

belief in Jesus Christ. As the chapter of life inevitably closes, I contemplate the urgency of seizing the day, leaving a legacy that echoes through eternity and sparks inspiration long after our final breath. Join me in this episode as we navigate these topics with sincerity and a longing for divine wisdom.

Good morning. It's Arlo Johnson in Vernon, British Columbia, coming to you at 10.15 am on March the 16th, and hopefully it's about spring. It'll be up to about 60 degrees Fahrenheit this afternoon, which is not bad, but it is the 16th of March, so it should be expected. So the goodness of spring, which I've said before, if you've listened to my podcast, is something that I actually really look forward to and I think everyone has in mind , not just me, I mean everyone actually looks forward to spring. When you see the activity that goes on around the different sites, I know what you call them gardening sites and whatever there's people just running around packing bags of this and bags of that, pots and all kinds of stuff every spring.

I think I mentioned this before and I'm going to mention it again the difference between what mankind thinks is the right way to learn things and God thinks the right way to learn things, and I think in all cases God is superior and God is right. For instance, spring in God's world starts around the 12th of this calendar called Abib, which I believe is around April in our calendar, so around the 12th of April, and it certainly starts out here and he said that's, but that's spring. But it's not just spring. That is the new year. The winter is over and now a new year and it's not like we do with January, the 1st at midnight in a snowbank somewhere on the highway in Saskatchewan. I mean, I can't follow that at all. God's day starts at sunset, the old day ends at sunset and a new day begins at sunset. Now there's also 30 days of the month every month, and the adjustment is made once every four years. Somehow I forget how it's done. But now, when you think about the way God's mind must work, or plan that works, and the way we do things where we're utterly, you know, we're inferior by far. God does things that are very common sense, and I mean let's place it as a race of people. We don't practice very much common sense. There's some people who do, I guess, but the majority do not. So I guess that's the life we have. Someday, I guess, we'll go by God's plan, God's rules.

It's very interesting, when you study this a little bit, that God has a plan and it's a plan and we are part of that plan and we're in that plan Every day we get up. We're part of that plan and it's another slice of time in that plan. The plan is, you know, it's not changeable, it's absolutely built into stone. Basically, you know, how long do you think in our time? Say, do you think God took the form that this plan was in this age on the earth and the different earth ages and now this earth age? It's like God was trying a few scenarios and he settled on this one and for some reason or other I certainly can't prove it or anything like that but it appears to me it's like we're in the final run of this plan. It's like this plan has been kind of run through once before and now we're in the final plan and that means that I am on here having a podcast and if you happen to listen to it, it means that that was part of the plan. That is how precise the plan is.

It has to be like that, because all of nature is built on a reducing scale. You know, like all the animals and all this stuff, they last for only so long. They're not permanent. And there's now, I think, thousands of species of animals gone. There's been species of humans too. But when God comes along and says or Jesus says I'm going to build a place, I'm going to prepare a place for you so that you can be with me.

Well, that puts things in a different light altogether. That means God has settled on a plan and God wants sons, he wants a big family and, let's face it, if we could grasp the level of magnitude that God deals with like he doesn't, he never exaggerates, never. He never embellishes anything. Every word he says is a powerful word. It's necessary to what he is saying and being that God is Almighty, you know, and he is a great spirit who can change or do anything, is most likely in the position where he deserves and what requires, the top, largest presence in the whole universe, because he, the universe, belongs to him, everything.

Now, if that's the case, the city of God which we know the size of is 1500 miles square, 1500 miles high, we can't visualize it. You can't remember how many floors or what it would be, 1500 miles up high, but what would be there? And basically, I certainly didn't know until just lately that the city wouldn't fit on this planet. I've never said anything about that. He just said I will create a new heaven and a new earth, and which means he's going to have an earth that is going to accommodate the size of the city. And to do that, from what I understand and what I've read these people have done calculations on it says that the world, this world's size, has to increase by 366 times. So instead of an 8,000 diameter world, 8,000 miles, 4,000 radius, but 8,000 diameter, it's going to have to be tons and tons better than that. But I guess the only way you can explain that is because this is where God is going to be. This is going to be his headquarters and we're going to live in his headquarters.

If we are in his book of life, that's the most important thing. All this other stuff and we have elections and we have this and we have that and we fight about this and argue about that None of that is really that important. I mean, it's kind of day-to-day important on a small scale, but what's really important is that if we are going to be in Christ's book of life, that is the thing I mean. You tell me if there's something more important for you or me. I'd like to hear it. But I know there isn't and I'm sure you know there isn't, and it depends on how much procrastination. We do or had, and I certainly know about that too, and I think it makes it really tough.

If you get to a point in your life where you actually believe what Jesus Christ has said and what's going to happen. He says this will happen and that will happen. You believe that, you finally believe it. And then you sit back and look at the world around you and you are Just about blown away when you see people who don't even know about it, think about it or do anything about that or even take it seriously and make you wonder. You know, I mean, I can't get anyone to do it, I Can't say you do this and you do that, and then you know you'll be in this kingdom. No, only God can do that. He's the only one that can call people to Christ, his son, who is going to be the judge of the world and who is going to be, who is the savior of the world and who is also God. The father, the son and the Holy Spirit make up God. I don't know if it ever bothers you or makes you wonder. When you look at somebody, do you actually say to yourself man, are they going to be in God's kingdom or not. The thing is I, you know, I personally totally believe what God says. I totally believe what Jesus Christ has said. It took me a long time to do that, but Once I did that, that was a big relief for me, because I could believe everything that Jesus Christ said and it cleared up a lot of things, a lot of things.

You know, I went to the Lutheran church for about 60 years, on and off, you know, not very often. During that time I never even heard about the book of Revelation. I Never even heard about these different things. I said right in the Bible. I mean why did I take catechism? I was confirmed in the Lutheran church. Never Heard about it, told about. It Was always these fluff things sort of like Traditionals, traditions, you do this, you do that and and you know nobody bad in the kind of Lutheran church or anything like that. They're all good, that's. I don't think they're good for people. I'm good for people Because they are like milk toast. They're weak and they don't seem to Form up or have a stance on things. That's not good.

When I read about the Catholic Church, I just think to myself. You know, the largest church, the largest Christian church anyway, on the planet, and it is when you read what they are and what they've done and what they believe and what they've changed. And they said not to change things, and they say, oh we can change. You know, to me they're just. Here's a preview of the Antichrist Church, which I think they're going to be False prophet or whatever it's called. I can't see that. Their whole deal. You know, taking the place of you know they say that they are the priests who can forgive sins and all that sort of stuff. No, I don't think they can. The Pope is infallible now.

 People are told, that's what they saw on the news, and they cannot separate the facts that the news is not. It's not trustworthy. You can't believe the news anymore. It is so slanted.

And so the whole deal is basically the description of Satan, who takes the truth and then puts a lie in it. He twisted it. That's how he sells the lie, and I think it's a good thing that he's been judged, which he has. Satan has been judged already and he's waiting for his first go in the hole for a thousand years. And you know, you can see why God is going to let him out because he's going to gather up all the people who still are against God, against everything. There'll still be people like that. He's going to gather them all up and then that's going to be the wiping that's going to clean again. Yes, it's a plan. There's no doubt about that. One of the mysteries really is who is going to be in the kingdom of God forever. You know, Jesus said there are those who will be the greatest in the kingdom and those who will be the least.

When I read that and thought about that for a while, I thought you know, that opens up a whole big thing. There's a hierarchy there of some kind. Then there's the big city, huge, huge city, and the earth way bigger than it is now. Is there some way that this is going to make a situation where people will have to work their way out of something on outside the city, it's said, because outside the city are dogs and this, and that you know that's what it says. I'm not saying that, that's what it says. And yet the gates of the city are never closed, day or night. There is no day or night. There's only day, only daytime. There is no night, there is no time.

When people say that you live forever, well, I guess that's one way of saying it, but it is that you live where there's no time, there is no time, and you have an indestructible spiritual body that you live in. It's not physical, there's no blood veins, you don't go to the toilet, I don't think. And they still have. They have meat, they eat, I guess, or have banquets or something. I mean it's hard to figure out, isn't it? Well, I don't know if that's how it happens. I don't know if they say it's about banquets, but it could be some kind of a very important saying , so if you're like I am, if you're thinking that there may be a chance, that if you ask for forgiveness and believe in Jesus Christ and believe in

God, that there may be a chance that you may see the time when God will say to you go to the right and enjoy the things that God has provided for you, and hopefully not say, go to the left. I don't know you. That's well, that's going to be it.

And once a person dies, you can't actually do much about it anymore. He only can do something as long as he is physically and mentally alive. Once he dies, that is the end of his life. So you know, a person who doesn't want to really procrastinate forever can't guarantee it. Anyway, good thing that there's a way to do this. Only hopefully we have to do it and that hopefully, somebody will pay attention to that, I don't know. Anyway, thank you for listening and God bless you and we'll see you later.

Spring's Metaphors and Mars' Dreams in Our Philosophical Odyssey

Chapter 11

Have you ever found yourself wrapped in a blanket, watching the March winds whirl outside your window, and contemplating the grand mysteries of the universe? Join us on our latest podcast episode where we take a philosophical journey through the musings of life, the search for meaning, and the grand designs of faith. From the eager anticipation of spring's rebirth in Vernon, British Columbia, to the audacious plans of colonizing Mars with Elon Musk at the helm, we traverse topics that will stir your soul and challenge your beliefs. Witness how we dissect the essence of our fleeting existence and deliberate whether our environmental endeavors align with a higher divine plan, or if we're merely imposing our will upon it.

Feel the tension between societal norms and personal beliefs as we navigate through waters often muddied by religious doctrine. We'll unpack the true nature of goodness—and whether it's always in lockstep with what's popular—as well as the implications of a society drifting away from the fear of God. Observe the transformative power of natural cycles as metaphors for life and divine

1 harmony, and prepare to question everything you thought you knew about spirituality and
2 environmental consciousness. Let's seek clarity together in the messages of prophetic writings,
3 especially the enigmatic Book of Revelation, and ponder their significance in our world today. As
4 the seasons change, so too may our understanding of the world and the spiritual path laid before
5 us
6
7 .Well, good afternoon. 2.42pm in Vernon, British Columbia, it's pretty chilly for March. I mean, it's
8 not cold or anything, but it's a cold breeze Waiting for spring. That's what I'm waiting for, and that's
9 for sure. Anyway, I hope you're all doing well and that you're glad that winter is just about over,
10 and so I'd like to spiel off a little bit today about wisdom or the lack of it.
11
12 You know, I was watching Elon Musk here talking about stuff here just a few minutes ago. It
13 triggered me into thinking. You know, you can be as educated as you like, you can do all kinds of
14 things and you don't really know why you're here. And many people don't know why they're here.
15 They don't even think about why they're here. You know he says we have to go to Mars. You
16 know, keep civilization going in case the earth goes bad, and blah, I don't agree with that. I don't
17 agree with that because you know, if people haven't finished exploring this planet, much less Mars
18 ,I could see going to the moon doing stuff there. You know, if there's a reason, they could use it for
19 something that's just like next door.You know, we've been there. It can be done, that's not a
20 problem. Go there and come back, and so what I'm getting at is people don't understand the
21 reason we are here.
22
23 Most people, it seems to me, don't grasp the idea that this is a temporary life. You're here for a
24 reason to make up your mind about God. One way or the other, God has given you this
25 opportunity. Everything that God does is among the scale compared to us, you know, it's like
26 standing in a hallway and looking down at a little speck that you can barely see on the floor, and
27 then that would be us looking up at God, who would be many times that. The thing is. Everything
28 God does is such a scale that I mean it's pretty hard to follow it and understand it. Do you
29 remember Jesus said I go to prepare a place for you that where I am, you can be also. Now when
30 you read what it is, and you can read it as well as I can 1200 stadia, 1500 miles square, 1500
31 miles high. You can't even imagine a city that size. The other thing that should blow your mind is
32 that, according to revelation, all the stuff in this great city is slanted and directed towards Israelites,
33 naming things like gates, stairs, whatever, foundations 12 tribes of Israel, 12 steps, 12 gates, 12
34 tribes of Israel, the lost 12 tribes of Israel? Basically not 12,. It was 10.

1

2 Now you say, you know, God is not going to say, oh, we can't just have Israel, lights here in this
3 kingdom, oh God, no, we have to make sure we have diversity, I doubt it. I don't think he is even
4 talking or saying that. He would be so diverse you couldn't get to verse, because he's made
5 everything that way. Here it's like you know, if one group thinks they're better than another and
6 whatever, all of a sudden we have to be so holy and so good that we've got to have these other
7 people to come in and you know, we'll have to cut down for whatever. Yeah, well, maybe I don't
8 know if that's it. I do know God deals with that much better than we ever could.
9

10 Well, the thing is that people who plan for the protection of the environment and to make sure that
11 the earth survives forever, they're going against God's plan. God's the one that has the plan. God's
12 the one that decides the plan, not his little minions that he created. But that's what it is and it's
13 getting sort of. You won't say anything against that you could be in jail. You shouldn't be able to
14 say anything, you shouldn't be able to be on the internet, because we don't like you saying things
15 like that. And well, you know the thing is I can't really describe it to you, but it seems to me that you
16 know this planet is going to be dissolved by fire, purified and renewed. That's it. I make a new
17 heaven and a new earth. He forgot to tell us how big he's going to make it, but obviously he's
18 going to have to be way bigger than this planet, because his city wouldn't fit on it, otherwise, you
19 know, you gotta put that in your pipe and smoke it.
20

21 Now the thing is that the whole world more or less every day is getting in your face, like you know,
22 it has lost any fear of God, that's for sure. That's a pretty big thing. You know what's the result of
23 that going to be? They don't fear the creator of the universe, who created them and everything
24 else and who has set up laws and rules and plans that he's going to do, and he's asking you to go
25 along with it and believe him and live in a world, a new world with him forever, for instance, this
26 new world that he's talking about, the new kingdom, I don't imagine there's anything like money.
27

28 There wouldn't be any money, no money whatsoever, and I guess there's no reason to have
29 money. Everything you wanted would be around you or wherever else all the time. That's hard to
30 grasp, isn't it? No money, no, two races and none of that, just one group of sons that he says that
31 he wants as a family. That's his plan, because he wants them to do things with him gladly and
32 fairly, a hundred percent, and a lot of it is, worship type things or something.
33

1 No time, there's no more time. Time doesn't exist in that world, there's no such time. I honestly
2 think it's like Time is like the present time all the time. You're just in time. All the time that is.
3 There's no time like we have. There's no today, tomorrow and this afternoon. Everything's now.
4 That's hard to grasp, things like that, isn't it? If the old brain, working as hard as you like, it's still
5 hard to get around it. But the thing is there is so much that God has to actually show his children,
6 his sons, That's most likely no end of these things, these are most likely unlimited. Now, if that's
7 something to look forward to, you know this, life just pales in comparison. It really does.
8
9 Now people say things like to be a good person, you should not discriminate against anyone. So
10 that's most likely true in one sense. But if you don't discriminate against somebody who does
11 something that you don't believe in, not because you don't believe in it, but because God does not
12 believe in it and God does not like it. If you Fuzz that over and say, oh, I've got to be a good guy,
13 I've got to love everyone you know everybody.You are going to be on your own. He is not going to
14 protect you and Make sure he waits for a long time. Let people try to get around it. I'm actually
15 afraid to be the way the world wants you to be, because if you do that, if you want to be the way
16 the world wants you to be, you are not going to be in line with what God wants you to be.How
17 about clothing? You won't be taking anything absolutely nothing. Are you starting to get nervous
18 about all this ? Is it too big a deal to handle ?
19 It is a good thing to meditate about a future of Joy and true happiness. And take time to thank God
20 the Father and Jesus for such a great plan.
21
22 Now, who's the winner? Who's the big boss? Who's got all the power? Not the world. Lots of
23 people around you ,You see them die, born and die every day. They come and go. That's it. That's
24 what you're going to follow. Well then, you've got a pretty shallow deal, you know, yeah, it's
25 amazing when I think about it, when Jesus said I go to prepare a place for you, and then you read
26 what this place is, who said, that Jesus is the Creator, the Word spoke and it was so. All things
27 were created by Him, all things.
28
29 We're coming up to spring sometime soon now, I don't know, maybe in the Jewish calendar or
30 something like that? I guess that's what it is, the 12th of Abeb is like April 10th, 12th of April in this
31 calendar. That's the start of a new year, not just spring, it's the start of the new year. But he
32 considers the start of a new year to be the start of new nature, growth, and life. That's when the
33 new year starts. The old year is over, it was dead in the winter and it's coming to life again. And
34 when it comes to life he says that's spring. Now I can believe that and I can agree with that really.

Just like when it gets to be about 6pm tonight, it'll be sunset. That means this day is over, according to God, and a new day starts. I can't argue with that. That makes way too much sense to me.

The things that God does and preaches and writes about and says in his plan are things that are actually very simple. They're not fancy things to try to figure out. They're very down to earth, simple, and it's man who twists everything wrong and makes it complicated. That's a fact, it really does. And the way the world goes and the way it's going to go is well, it's an amazing thing. If you actually take the time to figure out what's going to happen and read what the plan is, all you gotta do is read the book of Revelation. Really, Jesus Christ lays it all out for you and it's there, and I think that's a pretty interesting time of life to be alive.

I don't know how soon it's going to happen. I'm pretty sure it's going to drag out for a while yet, because things are going to get so bad. There's just absolutely no excuse anymore. Not one bit, , but anyway, the good thing to look forward to is that it's spring. I will be 90,on April 22nd. That's not too far from now and I guess I have to look forward to that. You know, then, what's going to happen. You know what comes after 90, 91? I don't know. We'll find out, and that's the one thing about it. We all will find out. With that, I'm going to say good night, goodbye, and God bless you.

Exploring Eternity and Earthly Transitions: Reflections on the Universe, Family Dynamics, and Christian Hope

Chapter 12

Ever pondered the vastness of the universe and the fleeting nature of our mortal coil? Come take a journey with me, Arlo Johnson, and my guest as we unwrap the mysteries of existence and the biblical vision of a new heaven and a new earth. Our conversation spans the impermanence of the present world, the grand scale of divine architecture as envisioned in Revelation, and the inclusive

1 nature of salvation. We ask not just about the size of God's city, but the weight of our choices in a
2 world where life is but a precursor to eternity.
3
4 Transitioning from celestial to societal, we examine the seismic shifts in family life, the waning of
5 time-honored traditions, and the societal implications of changes in gender roles and fashion. With
6 a keen eye on the transformation of community structures, especially within the agricultural
7 heartlands, we explore the potential for societal upheaval and the resilience required in times of
8 adversity. This episode culminates with a contemplation of Christian eschatology, discussing the
9 tribulation, the second coming, and the puzzle of faith in the modern world. Join us for this episode
10 and emerge with a renewed perspective on the world around you and the world to come.
11
12
13 Good afternoon. This is Arlo Johnson, coming to you from Vernon, British Columbia, at about 3 pm
14 on Saturday, the 24th of February. Hope everything's finding you well and that things are okay
15 where you are. So I started thinking about a couple of things, and one of them was the idea that
16 you know that things are permanent and all this stuff and nothing changes. And you know. It really
17 really is not true. Everything changes really.
18
19 But what I'm going to mention and God says is I think it's in Revelation or someplace that I make
20 everything new. I make a new heaven and a new earth, and in the new earth there will be no sea.
21 That's quite a bit to swallow right there. I mentioned this before. I didn't pay really much attention to
22 that and I don't think most people do. I'm going to create a new heaven and a new earth. That
23 means that this is not permanent. We're on a temporary deal and that's got to resonate somehow.
24 After all, we don't own anything. We're just here and we're here for just a short period of time. Now,
25 when God says I create a new heaven and a new earth, he doesn't say what kind of an earth,
26 bigger earth, smaller earth, whatever but there will be no sea. It's like you got to look at some clues
27 here to figure out what's going to happen.
28
29 In the book of Revelation it's discussed in chapter 20 or something like that, verse 20, I think it's
30 called chapter 20, that the city of God that Jesus said that he's building and that it will descend on
31 this planet. Now, right, here you've got to stop and say, well, now I believe everything that God
32 says and what Jesus said. I believe every single word of it. The only thing I've got to understand is
33 what he's saying. And this city of God is so large, so big that it wouldn't fit In this planet we live on
34 now. It wouldn't fit in the continental United States, from the Canadian border to the Caribbean

1 Sea or not the Caribbean Sea, but the Gulf couldn't fit. It'd be hanging over the Gulf. Now,
2 according to the size of this planet, and this planet is not that big, it really isn't 4,000 mile radius
3 8,000 mile diameter, and so it won't fit on this plane. God never said it won't fit. He just said this is
4 the planet, the city that I'm going to bring down. I don't know if it's going to be the city of God. He
5 didn't say where it was going to land.
6
7 The Earth would take what size to be for that city to sit on a flat plane On this planet? The north
8 and south gates would be 70 miles off the surface because of the curvature of the earth. It's such a
9 big city that on this planet it's too big for this planet.
10
11 It is saying that this is temporary. This is temporary. You're on a temporary planet for a reason.
12 Make up your mind which one you're going to choose. Well, I'm giving you a chance to be a
13 permanent person. Right now you're not. You're not a permanent person because you, you're born
14 on this planet as a Physical person and you wear out and you die.
15
16 During that period, you have the opportunity to make a decision greater than yourself by far, and I
17 have to say that I learned I didn't learn it, I, I knew it somehow when I was about 15 years old and I
18 remember that plainly that I said to myself, you know, I was wondering about things like that at that
19 age and I said you know, it's got to be that I'm here to make a decision about something, and I
20 imagine I knew it was a decision about God and who God was. Because I'm 15, I've been going to
21 church and Sunday school and stuff like that for years. So I guess you know, I imagine that's why
22 I'm talking like this today. That's because I Went to Sunday school by myself with my pony and
23 buggy by myself. So it must have been a reason for it. I don't know, but I'm quite sure there was
24 and I'm quite glad it was.
25
26
27 I realize how temporary we are, very temporary, I mean. You know you can be here one day, gone
28 the next, it seems like, and that most happens every day to someone. I see you all around me, but
29 I hear you realize that that comes to somebody's death. For instance, let's say, did you hear
30 George died? Oh no, is that right? Oh, my gosh, George died. When did he die? Uh, the day
31 before yesterday. Oh, that's too bad. Oh, yeah, uh, yeah, uh, could you pass the potatoes please?
32
33 I said, well, as long as people care about that, because it doesn't happen to them, it happens to
34 someone else. I mean, that's what people think. I mean they don't think so.That's how the mind

works, you know.I shouldn't say, imagine God laughs at the things that happen to people and what people do I'm quite sure he does and uh, to think that he went through all this trouble just to have sons.

That's the whole thing. There's no other reason for this world than everything else. God wanted sons and I think, uh, women are a little jealous at the fact that he wanted sons. Well, there's a good reason for that. God does not want two different sexes to live forever in his kingdom, to be fighting, battling and jealousy. Doesn't need it, doesn't want it, doesn't need the womb. There's no more births, and so the women will not be going to heaven as women or be reborn into his kingdom. They will be reborn the same as if I went there. They will be the same If I'm reborn. I'm not going to be the same as I am. It's going to be a different kind of person. What I've seen or read in some places, that the sons of God will be roughly like 20, 22 year old males roughly, and that's the age and whatever I guess most of them will look like. And so what's hard about that? You just go there. That's what you're reborn to. That too, same as the man, both reborn, not the same as they are on the planet Earth. But you can bet that there will be a lot of women who won't like anybody saying that, even if they know in their heart that that most likely is true.

I said to somebody today at noon looking around in the dining room and I said you know, there's no women wearing dresses in this room. There's no women basically doing their hair up, except there's a few that have a permanent or some kind. And I said they're all wearing pants, men, same as men. And I said I don't know, I guess it's handier. They think it's handier that way, like the only thing they do is they pull their hair up in a bun at the back and put a rubber band around it and call it good. They all do that. Now how should they? All but 90%? And you know, when I grew up, people, especially women, looked after themselves. They had curled up hair, stuff, whatever dresses and dressed up. And you know they were treated differently too.

Yes, god even says that women are not to wear men's clothes.

I don't think too many people pay attention to that, do you?

You know? But it says don't do it, You're supposed to be separate and different, which you are. And now you're jealous of men. I want to prove that you're the same as men. Well, good, but that gets into me. It's such a common thing that now a woman with a dress looks out of place practically. It sure looks a lot better.

1
2 Anyway, things change. That's why everything changes, and I don't think, I think, over the period of
3 time that I've been around, I can't say that a lot of things have changed for the better they're
4 not.They've changed more for convenience or you know, style, I guess you could say, or whatever,
5 but usually no, homes and families have not improved. That's why they've gone down. There's no
6 more real families. Well, I mean, there's bound to be some, but on a scale it is just about nil.
7
8 You know, I see it in my own background, in my own family. We had big families when I grew up.
9 Now they're just dispersed and gone. Most of them are not getting married anymore, they're living
10 with each other in fornacation. There's gays and there's whatever, and there's no big families
11 anymore, none at all. I can go back out now, which I'm going to do in April if I can make it and it's
12 less and less about what I call a family community. Less and less and less, the older people are
13 just disappearing and the younger ones aren't doing the same. They don't keep the same kind of
14 family Farming communities.
15
16 It's not as bad as in cities. Farming communities still try to have a family of some kind, I believe.
17 I'm quite sure, because it's conducive to having a family. But I think we're seeing the last edges of
18 family life, that's for sure. I've always visualized a thing where things get so bad that people revert
19 back to, like the survival of the fittest. People just come and take whatever they want from anybody
20 else and say go to hell. And I think that will happen Because there's things happening already. We
21 don't have the clue that we'd have a food shortage or something like that. It can happen. Things
22 can certainly happen in this country too, sad to say.
23
24 But hopefully all this will be over in a short time because nothing's come up yet. The bell hasn't
25 rung yet. When the bell rings, you know you've got seven years and that's the end of it. I mean,
26 that's seven years and that you're going to be in the tribulation when it starts. And you had to go
27 through seven years. The first three and a half are supposed to be very good, because the
28 antichrist is going to lie his way around and do all the stuff until he's got everybody where he wants
29 them, and then he's going to put the hammer down and then it's the real tribulation. And once
30 that's done, it's all finished. This earth part is all finished.
31
32 Christ comes back and puts a damper on everything, rearranges everything for a thousand years,
33 and if you're one of the ones who is resurrected at Christ's return, you'll be working under him,
34 with him and for him. Not a bad job, a good job. Well, here's hoping to see you in the employment

1 lineup. You never know. It's been offered. It's there for people to accept and it's hard for me to
2 think how people can refuse. That's what's really hard. But anyway, time to go, time to say
3 goodbye. I'll see you again in the meantime. God bless you.
4

Rebirth at Eighty-Four: Contemplations on Wealth, Faith, and Second Chances

Chapter 13

10 Gazing out at the snow-dusted trees of Vernon, I'm struck by the profound contrasts of our world—
11 contrasts that echo through my reflections on spirituality and material wealth. In the heart of this
12 episode, I invite you on a journey from the wintry calm of British Columbia to the sun-soaked luxury
13 of Los Angeles golf courses, revealing how these landscapes shape my perspective on life's
14 deeper truths. As I contemplate the economic allure and potential excesses of the golfing elite, a
15 thread of introspection weaves through our discussion, questioning the very nature of ownership
16 and the fleeting grip we have on our earthly treasures. Through a candid window into my own
17 experiences, I explore the Christian ethos that suggests we are mere stewards of the divine, a
18 view that underpins my personal narrative of transformation.
19
20 The waters of baptism symbolize a new beginning, a sentiment that resonates deeply as I share
21 the poignant moment of my immersion at the age of 84. The act, profound in its simplicity, marked
22 a turning point—a rebirth and a washing away of past missteps. Here, the essence of faith and the
23 journey toward eternal life take center stage. I challenge the metaphorical weight of infant
24 christening and advocate for a conscious, adult decision to embrace the teachings of Jesus Christ.
25 It's a conversation that beckons you to reflect on your own convictions, to consider the steps one
26 must take toward redemption, and the ceaseless quest for everlasting life.
27
28 Good morning. It's about 11 am in Vernon, British Columbia, about zero degrees outside. Getting
29 close to the end of February, it won't be long before we'll be looking at green grass again. That's
30 the welcome deal, I'll tell you. Sure is Well.
31

1 You know, I've been spending some time, in fact yesterday and today, watching golf tournaments,
2 especially on GolfPro on TV, and right now they're playing in Los Angeles. The other day that
3 we're playing and I forget where it was. What I'm getting at is when we're sitting here in the winter
4 time, usually there's some snow around and you know it's pretty chilly. And I'm watching this big
5 screen with the green and green and more green, and I'm looking at it and I'm just wondering to
6 myself how much do the people that are there appreciate where they are? You know, I imagine,
7 they do. But you know I can watch that game all day because it's a moving thing and you're
8 visualizing the whole thing. It kills a lot of time, I'll tell you. But what I'm getting at is how beautiful
9 the countryside there is and the golf courses are. I mean, you couldn't get greener grass, you
10 couldn't get more manicured lawns, you couldn't get more big, beautiful buildings. And when I
11 watch the amount of people, thousands, many, many thousands watching each one play. Now
12 they're a couple hundred feet away I can't see, I don't. I don't know if they can even see who's
13 playing, but they seem to, because they cheer and they let go and cheer again and they must pay
14 to go there. Mind you, somebody must pay something because you know, these purses are
15 Ludwig Hovland, I mean one FedEx Cup here just a couple weeks ago, 18 million. Nick Taylor, the
16 other day, one, forget that. Oh yeah, the Phoenix Open 8.8 million. And all those dollars have to
17 come from somewhere and there has to be a lot more than that to be able to pay people off. And
18 besides that, they don't just pay the first guy, they paid down to about 30.
19
20 Yeah, I missed my calling. I should have been a golf player. I should have played golf, darn right.
21 But I played little golf, but I didn't take it seriously, nothing, and you know, never even thought of it.
22 But anyway, when I look at those green, beautiful golf courses, I'm wondering how much people
23 are swayed by that. I'm looking at it and say, oh, isn't that beautiful? Well, it is. But you know
24 there's a danger. There's a danger in people idolizing the world or whatever and saying, oh, all this
25 is wonderful here and wonderful there. Places are pretty wonderful. Now, a lot of places are not.
26
27 God said don't be enamored by this world, you're just traveling through and don't love the world.
28 You can be in the world but you're not supposed to be of the world. And that's a tricky thing to
29 understand. But I kind of think I understand it because God is a jealous God. I guess that's why
30 Nothing that can do both that or you can do both, and everything is His, everything. To get that
31 straight in your mind takes a little dancing around. I'll tell you , you belong to Him. The cattle on the
32 Thousand Hills belong to Him, everything belongs to Him.
33

1 That's a hard pill to swallow because it means that you don't own anything. Not really. You're here
2 by the grace of God, that's it. I don't own this body, I mean, Women say that it's my body and I can
3 do what I like with it. Not true. There's no more of your body than a tree is.
4
5 And you know, it's a tough deal to try to understand what the person has to do to get through this
6 life and possibly into the next. And it's going to be a pretty slim deal because there are certain
7 things you've got to do or there's not going to happen. And one of the main things you have to do
8 is get to the point where you believe what Jesus said and you believe what God said Totally, no
9 reservations, no doubts, no nothing, just absolutely. You believe every word. Yeah, that's one
10 thing. The other thing I was saying about it the other day I was watching some programs on TV
11 and how important that baptism actually is. I don't think it's necessarily a salvation thing, but in
12 every instant when Jesus said, here's what you do, you believe and be baptized. Because if you're
13 baptized, God looks at that as you dying and when you come out of that you're a new person. And
14 if you're dying, that means everything that you ever did in your life up to that point has been buried,
15 no longer visible to God.
16
17 Oh, wow, you know I got baptized when, I don't know 84 or something like that, and I thought
18 about it. You know, after 84 years I've piled up a lot of things that most likely shouldn't have done.
19 And let's get baptized, I said and I Will, I think I've mentioned this before, but you know, I sat there
20 and I thought about it and I thought, how about gonna get baptized? And Then I actually asked
21 God to supply this guy to do it. It was a fairly young guy. He was the son of a person that I sold a
22 house to, who was a house painter, and he painted like 120 houses there for me and His son. You
23 know, now he's a you know contractor for Big contractor actually, but he's about 35. I guess or
24 something like that, maybe 40 for all I know. But anyway he sort of preaches a little bit at the
25 Seventh Day Adventist Church in this one little valley, but he's not a preacher, he's just a speaker,
26 but he's right into it. So anyway, I asked God. I said, would you have him call me and Agree to
27 baptize me in the pool here? That's cool. You know, I built that Rex, and it was a pool in it. I
28 thought it was a good thing to use. So I just waited, I kind of, you know, thought about it but kind of
29 forgot about it. I think maybe About two weeks went by or maybe a little more, and I got a call one
30 night about seven o'clock at night and the guy called and he said hi, how are you doing?
31
32 I said fine, yeah. He said it's Paul here. Oh, I said how are you doing, paul? Well, he said not,
33 yeah, pretty good, yeah, I'm doing fine. I said do you know why you called me? No, he says I really
34 don't know. He said I just felt I had to call you. So I said well, you know what? I Would like to get

baptized and I want you to do it, and I'd like you to do it some Saturday morning about 8 am and I'd meet you here at the rec center and we'll go in and use the pool and Whatever. And I said give you a day or two to think about it. You know, let me know.

About two days later he phones back and he says Okay, he says I'll do it and Is this Saturday? Okay? I said yeah, fine. So he came out, baptized me on Saturday, went back to the office and talked and visited for a while. His wife and his daughter's small daughter were there. Anyway, that's what happened there and right until this day I'm glad I got baptized because you know I had, I did things when I was younger that I, you know, not proud of, and then you know, nobody really knows about it or anything.

But I often wonder about people, if they think about that, how important that maybe is to them. It's not. I don't believe that it overrides the fact that if you believe in Jesus Christ, like he said, you would have eternal life.

But he did say become baptized. So you know I'm the only one in my family who's baptized. The rest have been sprinkled. You know, when there were babies christened, a lot of them considered that to be baptized. But what good is that? They haven't done anything. They haven't got anything to wash away our sins to be covered.

So you know that's a Catholic thing, and I don't believe in that at all. I think you have to be an adult person to be baptized, and there's a few things that God requires not the, that you have to jump up and do all the time, but mostly they're spiritual things due to the fact that he wants you to believe exactly what he did and why he came here and who sent him here and why and you have to, do that before you qualify in his, in his way. Well, anyway, that's just a little blurb today. I'd like to just leave you with that, and the thing is, think about it. I can't do anything for you, that's for sure, and you'd have to do this on your own, and I'd like you, you know, if you do, let me know. I'd appreciate it if you did. Anyway, that's it for now.
to recognize the personal journey that is faith. Join me as we navigate the sacred waters of belief, the enduring promise of baptism, and the ceaseless quest for everlasting life.

Contemplating the Sacred and the Secular in Life's Grand Tapestry

Chapter 14

As winter's chill thaws into the promise of spring, our latest episode finds me musing on the curious dance between eternal divine commandments and the mutable laws of humankind. With Vernon, British Columbia's gentle winter as my backdrop, I explore the natural cycles that govern our lives and question the peculiar construction of our modern calendar. Why does it not sync with the celestial clockwork God has set in motion? The discussion unfolds to contrast the immutable nature of divine law with the ever-shifting landscape of human legislation, where laws are as transient as the political winds that shape them. I probe the sacred tenets of the Ten Commandments, critiquing the liberties taken by religious institutions in their interpretation, and reflect on the grand design God has for our existence, stretching beyond the simple act of procreation to the spiritual sons and daughters in His kingdom.

In a world where every moment is chronicled by a divine ledger, I share a profound personal experience that underscores the interconnectedness of our lives with the celestial narrative. My story—a revelation about the conception of my first son—serves as a testament to the belief that our lives unfold according to a preordained path within God's vast plan. As we tread through these spiritually charged discussions, we also delve into the significance of faith and hope, holding fast to the truths personified by Jesus Christ. I leave you with a message of spiritual tenacity, encouraging listeners to anchor themselves in the principles that elevate us above the terrestrial fray, and I extend a heartfelt blessing, hoping that our words may inspire reflection and bring a touch of grace to your journey.

Good evening. It's 8.15 pm in Vernon, British Columbia, where I'm speaking from, and it'll let me take just a quick look here.It's about right around freezing right now in Vernon, British Columbia, and, you know, not too bad. I mean, we're just about at the half point of February and it looks like it's going to be about like this right through the end of the month. If that's the case, we really had a pretty easy winter. I don't know what it's like we are at, but the thing I look forward to and I tell you I

1 really do as I get older, I look forward to more and more and I just sort of watch, watch it, and it's
2 like I don't know a big deal for me.
3
4 Our year starts on January the 1st in Canada, you know that's like saying it starts on January 1st
5 at 12 midnight in the snow bank in Saskatchewan, at 20 below. That's when our year starts. What
6 a dumb thing. Nothing we can do about it. You realize that God's calendar is totally different. This
7 would have been a new day. It would have started at around I don't know 5,:30 pm. God says the
8 day ends at sundown and a new day starts. Now can you argue with that? That's exactly what
9 happens, not at midnight. And then he says a new year starts around the 10th or 11th of April in
10 the month I think they call it Abebe. Now that to me would be also very reasonable. A new year
11 starts, winter is over, the green grass starts and there's the rebirth of another year. The sun goes
12 down. That's the end of that day. There's no more day left. You start a new day and it's dark and it
13 goes over and the sun comes up again in about 10 hours.
14
15 You know, it makes me really wonder that the human race thinks it can make laws. It really does. I
16 watched the Congress of the United States going out and talking on this and that the one side was
17 just ragging against the other side. Democrats have got one guy that just keeps on and the other
18 side rags right back and the next day they do it again. Now what kind of good does that? Do they
19 think that if they do that, people think they're doing a good job and will reelect them? Mistakes
20 they're making so that they allow them to be there too long. You know, every time they make a
21 law, very few times they make laws that are a good law. It might be good for one group or
22 something, but not for everybody. It's not a level law. Then they sort of water it down and change it
23 over years.
24
25 You know, when God said that if you eat in the garden of the tree of the good and evil you know
26 that you will die, well that's what happens we're all sentenced to death. We're all that are
27 sentenced to death on account of that. And it's simple. His law is absolute. There's no getting
28 around it. His law is so absolute that he had to allow his son to die in our place because his law
29 demanded it and his is a holy law, the law that would run the universe and everything else. He
30 can't change his own law just because you know. Something comes up and you know that's really
31 tough. It can't be a tougher penalty than that. If you break this law, you're dead, you're gone, you
32 die, you won't be around. That's a tough penalty. There's no tougher penalty than that. So when
33 God makes laws, the only thing if people would think about it and that you know, like really think
34 about it is that all his laws are for your and my benefit. First, forget what it is. The first four laws I

1 believe are four or five is to worship God and to follow his laws. The other six are how you treat
2 each other, how we treat each other in things, and that's the ten laws.
3 plan and he would be able to have sons.
4
5 Now he didn't say sons and daughters, he said sons. And the reason for that is that the business
6 of procreation and all that will be over and there's no way he would want two sexes living forever in
7 his kingdom, because look at the problem on earth with it Fighting, it's not all that time the womb is
8 not required anymore. So his plan is for sons. He wants many sons. Now, if you think about God
9 and his production of the universe, of things in the universe, when he makes flowers on a field,
10 how many does he make? That's unlimited practically. The stars you can't count the stars and yet
11 he claims he calls them by name. Now the thing is, you know, that's quite a thing, the idea that you
12 know he would do this to have sons.
13
14 He wanted sons and Adam was his first son, so he called him the son of God, and so that means
15 we're in the form of Adam. Adam wasn't just created, he was formed and set. He formed Adam out
16 of the dust of the ground and blew in his nostrils the breath of life. He was formed. I'm sure that
17 you and I are the same form, totally as Adam. Now you know, if you're a woman listening to this,
18 you say what are you talking about? That's exactly what I'm talking about, whether people like it or
19 not.
20
21 But here's the thing: a woman has just as much chance of being in the kingdom of God as a man
22 has. The only thing is she won't be a woman. She will be the same as the man, being there as a
23 son of God, I can't see anything wrong with that. Why would anybody complain about that? When
24 woman was created, to be a help meet for man and carry the womb and reproduce. Now, let's face
25 it, a woman has reproduced a lot, this world has been populated with eight billion people.
26
27 Now this is all done automatically. God has such a system, a place, that we don't even realize it's
28 so automatic, on autopilot. I mean, God doesn't come along and say you got to create another
29 child tonight at 8 o'clock to night. He puts in an urge into the men that basically add into the
30 women. But basically I think it's a stronger urge in men and they want to plant the seed and the
31 better looking the woman is, the more they want to plant the seed. Now they don't have anything to
32 do with it except the little muscular mechanics they go through. It's all automatic. They carry the
33 seed, they don't realize they have 10,000 sperm in them, most likely a lot more. But in these sperm

each one could create another human being. Many are spilled and gone and whatever Many go in at a time.

I would imagine there's a whole bunch of sperm that goes in in one ejaculation and only one gets into the egg. It has to hit it just right to cut, make its various head go in there and leave the information it carries for the next human being, because the egg is the feeding area that will feed the sperm and create cells and there's enough in that egg that the woman has that most likely does a whole bunch, most likely lasts for quite a while, Because it has to last until the child is being formed and can form blood vessels and whatever else. Otherwise it wouldn't be able to. But what I'm getting at it, it's all done automatically. The woman doesn't decide to build blood vessels, she doesn't decide how he's going to be fed or whatever else. The man doesn't do anything except plant the seed. He's never seen the seed, he doesn't know what it is, but he has it.

Now you talk about an automatic system to create all kinds of humans that God loves. You know, the thing is that there is something in the humans that God puts in at the moment of conception and that is the human spirit he receives. That's the automatic thing that happens. That spirit stays with the person all his life and I believe that spirit is connected to some kind of system that records every breath that the person takes, every thought. Everything is recorded somehow, and when you die and you outlive your life, that returns to who put it there. It's like it's back to God and it's like just come back and talk it away, or the resurrection, when it'll be called up again.

Now, I didn't come up with that plan, did you? No, we didn't have anything to do with it at all. And you know, it's funny how some things work. I remember when we were on a trip to Saskatchewan one time ,it was in the fall fall , and we didn't have any kids with us my wife and I just took off to Saskatchewan to visit a guy that used to work with me and anyway we were upstairs in their upstairs bedroom where we were staying there overnight and my wife and I we basically had sex. But that's the only time, only time, that it hit me and it was like as soon as that act was over I just kind of stopped and I said, oh, this is going to be a child I didn't know it was going to be a son, but I knew at that moment that she was going to be pregnant, I knew that whatever had been done right there, and it just happened like two minutes afterwards, five minutes afterwards maybe, and it was like you know, when I'm trying to explain this and I think you may be known this there are times when something happens to you that it makes you stop and you wonder what happened? Is that what happened? What happened? And I realized I knew that there was going to be a child right there. I didn't know what happened to my son and why that was. I don't know why. I really don't know. That must be my first son and then we had another son.

1

2 But there's strange things that happen to everybody's life and I think a lot of it is how sensitive we
3 are to it. If we're not sensitive to it, it'll go by right over. Who knows? But there are other times
4 when it appears to be something, just like a spirit or a thought or something comes over you and
5 you know it. It's different, it's not the same. It stops you and you're cracked practically, and that's
6 something to kind of watch for, because things like that happen.
7
8 I believe that if you pray and talk to God, the Creator of the universe, which you're entitled to do
9 under the auspices of Jesus Christ, that's how you got to do it. You got to say I'm praying to you in
10 your son's name, Jesus Christ. That's how I come to you. That's the calling card that he has to
11 have Now. That's open right now. It's open tomorrow. It's open tonight. It's open the next day. It's
12 open 24 hours a day. There's no charge, and it's instant. It works instantly.
13
14 That means forever. Yeah, that's a long time, but imagine there are such depths of things that will
15 happen that you'll be totally, totally immersed in it and you never sleep. You never have to do
16 anything. You have life in you, total. You don't have to eat, you don't have to sleep, you don't sleep
17 as there's no night and you don't sleep anyway. You're, you're awake, and I wonder if you know
18 you're on, just like on duty, 24 hours a day, and then say 24 hours a day, there's no day there.
19 There is no day, it's just time. But there is no time anymore. It's God's time, which is now forever.
20 There's no midnight and morning and afternoon, none of that.
21
22 When you catch it, When you start to think about stuff like this and you catch it, playing it blows
23 your mind away, I'll tell you. It makes you think that you know a person really should be doing
24 better, trying to be doing the things that God requires. Well, anyway, we've gone over a few
25 minutes here. That's good enough, and I hope that the world's news is not getting you down. Don't
26 let it get you down. Doesn't matter. It's planned, it's gonna happen. Every single thing that happens
27 is all planned. I'm convinced of that. Totally planned, every single thing, and it'll progress along.
28 Some of it will be hated and some of it will be glad to see, but there will be a lot of things we won't
29 like to see.There will be moments we may have to suffer for it too, but anyway, I don't think it's
30 gonna be too dull. You know, I think it's a pretty exciting time coming up.
31
32 Regardless of what happens, it's the result in the end that counts.Thats what your hope is and
33 what you can believe. Your hope is and you can believe because God is the truth and Jesus Christ
34 is the truth. So I am the truth, the way and the life you can only come to the father through me,   I

don't think it hurts to mention that every so often, because you know we're like sheep we go astray
pretty easy and hard to keep us on track, that's for sure. Anyway, that's very good for today and I
would appreciate it if you stayed this long. You're, you're a good guy if you did that, a good girl if
you did that. But thank you very much for that and I would also like to say God bless you and I
hope he does. Thank you very much and good night.

Unraveling the Implications of Shifting Values in a Fractured Age

Chapter 15

As society's compass spins wildly, we confront the crumbling pillars of family values and religious
respect, promising to unearth the consequences these seismic shifts may have on our future.
Venture with us and discover the intricate tapestry of modern life, where the looming reign of King
Charles III mingles with ancient biblical prophecies, and the political battleground of the United
States is marred by polarization, with Donald Trump at its epicenter. Explore the potential
extremes that such divisions might foster, and the heralding of an era teetering on the precipice of
profound change.

We navigate the murky waters of an age potentially drawing to its close, marked by a biblical
seven-year countdown, and the ensuing cultural and generational struggles to secure life's
milestones against a backdrop of economic uncertainty. Listen as we dissect the growing divide
between the fortunes of business owners and their employees, foreshadowing a societal correction
on the horizon. In times where truth seems a rare commodity, we cling to the teachings of Jesus
Christ and God, emphasizing their wisdom as our steadfast guide through these turbulent waters.
Join us as we heed Jesus's stark warning against deception—an anchor in this storm, reminding
us that without his teachings, this life might be as good as it gets.

I'd like to kind of go over something. I think I've said this before, but you know, comparing over my
lifetime how things have changed. Like a lot of people don't think that it has changed, the life they

1 live, they believe, is always kind of been that way. Whether you're 18, 28, 58, it doesn't matter. But
2 after you know, I've lived from 1934 to 2024, a 10-year short of a century. Well, that's quite a while.
3
4 Things do change and, believe me, there's been no change for the better In mechanical and, you
5 know, material goods and stuff like that. That has changed, that has improved, new, whatever, I
6 mean great, great strides in that. But the family has deteriorated from what it used to be and
7 there's no fear of God by anybody, in very few less all the time. And the whole idea that there is a
8 judgment coming for the people on this plot just goes that way. Right now, if you're watching the
9 news and on the internet and all that, you have no means to separate out the BS and whatever is
10 actually happening In those cases. It's a little bit of both and you have to sift it out and if something
11 you know perseveres pretty long the same old line of doing this, doing that or doing this, or they're
12 doing that here or they're doing it over here too, Well that means there's a drift towards something
13 different, either up or down, and in most cases it's going down. Cities are going down, people are
14 starting to run cities with a total disregard for what used to be, you know, family-friendly cities and
15 stuff like that. Not anymore. No, it's getting worse. There's more devious and deadly things going
16 on in big cities, mostly in big cities than ever before. And you know, I've just shook my head a lot of
17 times and said how can this keep getting like this? You know this, what is this? Can't get worse
18 than this, can it? And I come to the conclusion yes, it can and it will. God will allow it to do that To
19 such an extent that he'll have to step in and stop people from absolutely destroying everything.
20 When you hear about things going on well, you could say high places or whatever.
21
22 I just heard the other day that King Charles, who took over from Queen Elizabeth after her death,
23 is about 75 years old and I understand that he's suffering now from cancer of the prostate and
24 being treated for that. Some people can get treated for it. There's been a lot of people dying from
25 prostate cancer as it spreads. For some reason I feel a little uncomfortable saying this, but that
26 doesn't surprise me, because I don't believe he is destined to be a great king or anything like that.
27 He's a fill-in. I'm just speculating this now. Don't take it, for I can't prove anything. I think that he will
28 expire and William, his son, will be the next king, most likely for the rest of the period of time that
29 affects people.
30
31 It says in the Bible that I don't know where it says it, but that there will always be a descendant of
32 King David on the throne. The only throne they can talk about that way is the English throne. The
33 English throne is supposed to be going all the way back to King David. The Bible claims that when
34 the New World starts and the people of this planet are separated out, it mostly talks about the 10

1 tribes of Israel, whatever they are, and that King David will be over them in this world to come
2 again. That's a different thing. It's just that there's a lot in the Bible that says things like this. That
3 makes me wonder and in amazement really, is this the people that are going to run the world in the
4 future? Who is going to be? The white race, the tribes of Israel, the 10 tribes of Israel who basically
5 must be the white race? That's who ended up in Europe and all over? I don't want to speculate too
6 much on that because it doesn't do me much good to do that, but to me, when the Bible talks
7 about, plainly upfront about things like that, maybe that's God's plan. You know, when Jesus was
8 born and they grew up in Israel, he said that he was born and he was here to do something for the
9 lost 10 tribes of Israel.
10
11 Anyway, putting that aside, I was listening to an interview on I don't know what news network it
12 was, but they were discussing the politics of the United States and how dire it is. They were
13 discussing the fact that the Democratic Party or the Left or whatever you want to call them, has
14 said they will not tolerate Donald Trump from being the next president of the United States, and he
15 was pointing out that they've tried every means of discrediting him, you know, in the public,
16 through courts and this and that They've got him I don't know how many different charges against
17 him now and he's fighting them all and he says, if that doesn't work, he said I believe he said they
18 will murder him. And then he says, just to make it look even, they'll murder the Democratic
19 president too. Now people will hear something like that and you'll say, ah, but I'll tell you, people do
20 not realize the depths of evil, I don't know what else to call it. It's just devilish stuff and that it has
21 grown to that point where some of them claim they want to destroy the population of theirs down to
22 500 million, from 8 billion, all kinds of things, and the people that are doing this. You know, it's not
23 that I can't believe that. I do believe it because of how evil people can be. Most people think they're
24 living in a nice little cow pasture, someplace where everything is just calm and nice. And you know,
25 you get up and you go to bed, and you get up and you go to bed and that's it. No, it's not, it's like a
26 cauldron of stuff, evil stuff. Now I would say that I'm not predicting this or anything else, but should
27 something like that happen, that would be one of the saddest things I think I would ever have to
28 live through with everyone else.
29
30 And you know exactly what will happen Once it starts. You know when the end of this age is. It's
31 seven years later, absolutely. Not until then. There's things that still have to happen for it to start,
32 according to the Bible anyway. But I mean, we're living in an age right now where Maybe it's not
33 possible to have a Governing system that is anywhere near fair or honest.
34

1 And the problem is, the gullibility of the public? When I look at people and I listen to people and I
2 watch them and I cannot believe that they are so naive. They don't have a clue. They honestly
3 don't. They talk like the things they have but they really don't. They can be swayed so easily. Yes,
4 it's not even funny. They can be lied to on Tuesday, be mad about it on Wednesday and believe it
5 again on Friday.
6
7 Now the population of this world is going down, countries are going down. Imagine Canada is.
8 Basically, I think you have to have 2.1 children per family, woman, whatever To keep the
9 population even and, I guess, growing a little bit. If you don't, you go the other way. You're going
10 down and I'm sure we're below that and the United States is below that. Japan is like 1.2 instead of
11 2.1 and the population is aging. Just the same as it's doing in Canada and certainly in the United
12 States, I mean in big strides in England, London, england. That's just that's why All these things
13 that it contributed to have caused it.
14
15 They finally caused it. You know you kill your own children, you bring in strangers. It causes it,
16 that's it. You've lost your country, you lost your culture, whatever, and it's your fault. Nobody's
17 done anything Now. They only do it because they believe something. Where that belief comes
18 from, well, that's what the person has to decide, because God does not promote that. So who does
19 promote that? Who is the influencer that does that? God plainly said that Satan is the influencer.
20 He can't really force you to do anything, but he can influence you to such an extent that you do it,
21 and I think that's scary.
22
23 But our lifespan is only so long. I don't know how it is. Mine has been lasting pretty good, but to me
24 we know that we are not going to live forever. We know that we are actually going to die and we all
25 know that Some of us never think about it that much, but it's a fact. We don't know when. We know
26 we're going to die, but we don't know when, not exactly and I suppose that's done for a reason. I
27 guess if we knew in real life I think it would be a lot different. Yeah, but the danger we're living in
28 now each day is getting a little more dangerous to personally and to the world, and it's driven by
29 politics and it's driven by evil that just increases in the heart of man and it's sad. My biggest
30 problem is it drives me nuts when I see them doing things like you know, doing bad things you
31 hear about and yet I can't do a thing about it and I should not let it do that because it just upsets
32 me.
33

1 The girl that works at the office out where I go said her son has moved home. He's 28 years old.
2 He was living with a girl. Her father gave her enough money to make a down payment and pay him
3 a condo, townhouse or something, and she's going to give him a certain amount of money and
4 he's going to move out because they're not going to live together anymore. So he can't afford rent
5 and he's working and he's got a fairly decent job in a way, not just a shovel job, he's got a fairly
6 good job but he's going to have to live at home again.
7
8 And I told her, I said that this really makes me mad. I hate that, that a young man like that has no
9 chance right now. This generation just doesn't have a chance. They can't buy a house, they can't
10 start a family, they can't do that because they can't afford it. There's no way. And in a way I'm
11 thinking to myself and I said to her in a way he might be lucky you know, times change better he
12 may be lucky that he hasn't bought a seven, eight hundred thousand dollar house and a seven
13 hundred thousand dollar mortgage, because I mean, how is he going to pay for it? And if my guess
14 is any good, I'm guessing that this will carry on for a while. It will still inflate and whatever still has
15 inflation and things will go up. But, like anything else, things will come to an end and there will be
16 an adjustment, because there's going to be an adjustment of some kind and it's going to be a
17 harsh one, I think, when an owner of a business is well, owners are not all businesses, but of fairly
18 large companies and whatever makes seven hundred times what their average employee makes,
19 so that you know by third of January they made more money than their employee makes all year.
20 That's not right. If left to its own do, left to its own events, it's going to balance out. It's going to
21 happen because something's going to give and it will have to level out.
22
23 So I would say to somebody that your only safety to tell the truth there is no other safety around is
24 to believe and believe what Jesus Christ and God has said Don't believe anybody else. I don't. I
25 don't believe anyone else anymore. I can't because they're deceived. If you remember, or if you've
26 never heard it before, I'll tell you right now.
27
28 That's the last thing that Jesus Christ said when he rose from this planet and was leaving. He said
29 to disciples and those that were watching him he said do not be deceived. Now, that's a pretty
30 strong warning. He said do not be deceived? In other words, what I've told you is the truth. Don't
31 believe something else. And that, I think, is the best advice anyone living in this time now can
32 have. That's if they take it and the chance for the most part is going to take. Trouble is they don't
33 realize they have no future. If you don't do that, there is no future for you, none, and that's it.. You
34 know, whatever you live now is the best you're going to get you better realize that. Anyway, that's

1 enough of that time to go for supper. So I would say thank you very much for listening and I would
2 like to ask God to bless you all, every single one of you, thank you.
3

Discovering the Priceless Nature of Eyesight and Unwavering Faith

6
7

Chapter 16
9
10 Embark with me, Arlo Johnson, on a heartfelt journey through Vernon's soft winter as we uncover
11 the remarkable intricacies of human sight. Imagine for a moment the sheer impossibility of another
12 being placing value on your eyes, offering millions for the gift of vision you possess. Through the
13 tale of a steadfast 92-year-old cowboy wrestling with macular degeneration, we'll explore the
14 profound connection between our eyes and brain, and marvel at the complexity that even the most
15 advanced technology can't replicate. I'll also share my own brush with the fragility of sight, how
16 cataract surgery ushered in a personal renaissance of perfect vision, and the gratitude for medical
17 marvels that renew our sense of wonder.
18
19 With the clarity of newfound sight, let's examine the boundless horizons faith in God's promises
20 can reveal. The multitude of churches and diversity in beliefs may seem a muddle, yet one
21 constant remains: our immeasurable worth in the eyes of the divine. This episode promises to fill
22 you with optimism, as we remember that each of us is considered priceless, far beyond the limits
23 of human valuation. I extend an open hand, inviting you to join me in this auditory embrace, where
24 we find solace in the truth of God and Jesus Christ, and celebrate the hope that comes from
25 believing in something greater than ourselves.
26
27 Good afternoon. It's Arlo Johnson from Vernon, British Columbia, at 12.50 pm on January the 25th
28 2024. Coming to you today and I hope I'm finding you well and no bad sickness or something If
29 there is. Hopefully you'll get a word soon. Our help is on the way.
30
31 Like they say, the winter is coming along quite well in Vernon, British Columbia, and I'm hooked on
32 the valley here. It's like 40 degrees Fahrenheit today, that's eight degrees above freezing. Snow is

1 disappearing and we had some real cold days, at least one and a half days minus 20, 25 degrees
2 below zero or two days, and then we had snow, most likely two feet of snow by now. Over that
3 period it's down. Most places are struck right now, so that could be a very welcome winter. If that's
4 the case, it's only another four or five days at the end of the month and then in February and who
5 knows, we've had people out golfing in February here before Could happen again. That means
6 we've had a really rough winter, a whole one and a half days of it, and that suits me just fine and I
7 don't know where you've been this winter, but hopefully you didn't have to shovel too much snow
8 and didn't get too cold. I wouldn't wish that on anyone? So anyway, I thought I would talk a little bit
9 today about when God said you are wonderfully and miraculously, made. He wasn't kidding.
10
11 For instance, there's a guy that sits next to me here at our table. He's on my left side, a very nice
12 guy. He's about 93, always dressed very well, but he's an old cowboy, and he doesn't give that up.
13 He has button down button shirts and western suits and stuff. He does something every day and
14 he prides himself in that. But he has a scooter in the shed here but he doesn't really like driving it
15 anymore because of his macular degeneration that's taking place. He's getting shots right in the
16 eye for it now, but anyway he can't see the edge of the sidewalk. He does know where it ends, so
17 he's scared to drive a scooter.
18
19 So what really made me think of this is I was reading something the other day about basically this
20 scenario. It comes along to you and says I want to buy your eyes, I'll give you ten million dollars for
21 them, but I want both of them. Do you agree or not? I'll give you ten million dollars and you would
22 most likely say no, I couldn't do that, so he could offer fifty million. You'd look at them and say can't
23 do that either. In other words, your eyes and my eyes are priceless. What about the rest of the
24 things? The eyes most likely are the most valuable thing this body has.
25
26 When you think about it, I forget how many nerve endings and stuff. The images register on the
27 back of the eye and the receptors on the back of the eye send signals to the brain and the brain
28 interprets these signals as an image and that's what you see, that's what your brain sees. Now
29 they claim that the eyes can't be transplanted. The cornea can be transplanted, but not the eye.
30 They say that there's a sort of a nerve center that goes from the eye back and connects to the
31 nerve that goes to the brain, but the main one is only about two inches long from the eye. This
32 connects to this channel, to the brain or whatever, but it's only about a fifth of an inch wide. But in
33 that channel there's about a million nerve deals going through there, different ones. So there is no
34 way that they can reconnect that.

1
2 Now how can that be? You know, it's just ridiculous, isn't it, when you think about it, for people to
3 say we just, you know, progressed from a frog or a monkey or whatever. That is so ridiculous. You
4 know we replicate and it's unbelievable how it happens. But a man sees a little tiny, little wiggly
5 seed that gets into a woman's egg and buries itself in there, carrying all this information. And how
6 does that happen? I had no idea. And it has the information to create another human being and
7 with a lot of time with the traits of the father. That comes from Skin color, you know, hair,
8 everything that's pretty distinctive. You know either, if you're a white male, you most likely have a
9 white son. If you're a black man, you almost likely have a black son, and it never fails.
10
11 Removing cataracts they peeled them off and put a different lens on there and I ended up on 2020
12 Vision Not bad, eh, they got clouded over with this film of some kind and all they did is peel that
13 off. How he did that, I don't know, but he did it one eye at a time and you know it wasn't painful
14 really or anything. I just had to keep it covered for a little while and use drops and stuff in there. But
15 I thought about it and I thought I was a little risky doing this. But I guess not really it's not such a
16 risky thing when they do something like that. They do it every day. It's not that something can't go
17 wrong, and then I guess they do once in a while kind of miss the mark a little, but they usually can
18 fix it.
19
20 But you know how to do something like that. You know the eye doctor. I go to an eye doctor, an
21 eye surgeon actually and he's a specialist. . A couple of times my bottom eyelid drops down and
22 you're looking at a red, open kind of eye. I mean it's a little awful. And he pulls it up. Well, I've done
23 it twice. My eyes start to look pretty red again. You might have to do it again. That's a, you know, a
24 fixer-upper deal Like this, this one, this one is still okay, but the other one the muscle got much
25 worse and it drops down.
26
27 I guess I've had a few adjustments. I had them go in and cut out and scrape out my prostate gland,
28 and that's kind of been 10 years ago now and still working okay, but that was quite a deal. And
29 then, unbeknownst to me, I well, basically I can't smell. I never have been able to smell. So if I,
30 when I was living alone, I'd have stuff in the fridge that, you know, even a dog wouldn't eat, but I
31 didn't know it. But I let something go too long and I ate it. I guess I think it was some meat or some
32 kind, and I got, you know, food poisoning. It's really what it was and I just couldn't quit.
33

1 I had to go to the hospital again to stop it and they did, and while I was in there, for some reason,
2 they were sending me to have a test here and an x-ray there and a CT scan here and a full body
3 scan there, bone scan. And I said what is all this? Why am I doing this? I just came in here
4 because I had a fricking diarrhea and they said we've got to send you to Kelowna. You're going to
5 have to have stents put in your heart.
6
7 You've got three aneurysms, You've got two aneurysms. One is not too bad, but the other one is
8 ready to blow. He said it's not bad, you've got to get in there right now. So you know what? They
9 made two little slits down in my crotch, one on each side. I don't know they made a three quarters
10 of an inch long , and they went up one side with, I guess, a camera light and whatever, the other
11 side with knives and whatever they do, and they blocked off or cut out this big artery that was
12 ready to blow and they ended up finding another one. So they put in three.
13
14 I didn't know anything about it. I was there. I don't know if I stayed overnight, I don't think so. I think
15 I was in there early in the morning and I went home in the evening and I had the operation, like you
16 know, at 9 o'clock in the morning or something, and I ended up with two band-aids down there,
17 that's it. And they just said be very careful, don't stretch too much or something, or it'll start
18 bleeding, so careful. And I thought how can you do this kind of stuff? How did you go in there, pull
19 the stents in there, and when they pull them apart, they get smaller and smaller, and when they
20 push them together, they get bigger and bigger, and then they lock them in there and then the
21 flesh or whatever grows into them and grows right into it and they're there. So repair has been
22 made and I think that's quite an advance or something. I mean really, you know how tricky it can
23 be. One goes in there and they do it on a screen.
24
25 Did I have an anesthetic? Yes, it was an anesthetic. When I had the prostate, they gave me a
26 local, or whatever it's called, in my back here somewhere and everything below that was frozen or
27 whatever. And did that ever take a long time to get out of there? I honestly felt like both my legs
28 were like 22 foot thick trees. They were so bulky and so heavy I couldn't move them. Oh my God.
29 But anyway, my evening is kind of drifted off, yeah.
30
31 So I guess, when I think back on it, I had a couple of things happen, nothing, you know, nothing in
32 particular, and I never gave a thought to it. I never wanted to say, oh, I got to have an operation, I
33 did nothing about it, nothing. So I've been lucky, I guess, very lucky. Things happened to make me

1 go to the hospital. At that time I didn't go to the heart specialist area there because I had diarrhea.
2 No, the diarrhea put me in the hospital.
3
4 So they found out I had a heart failure. The doctor did a report for me that I had to send away a
5 month ago and I looked at it before I sent it away, before I mailed it. And he suffered from COPD.
6 What are you talking about and also had heart failure, has back problems, you know, makes it
7 hard for him to walk sometimes. Well, that part's true. I didn't know I had COPD and I didn't know
8 that my heart had failed. But I guess he classed that aneurysm deal as a failure.
9
10 I had to go ahead and repair the heart. Now, you know, when my dad was growing up, years ago,
11 well over 100 years ago, who wouldn't have that? Couldn't have done that. That's quite a thing how
12 things change. Thank you, I'm very glad of that. But you know, I'm glad that they did it and it was
13 no great discomfort to me to fix something like that.
14
15 But I, uh, I don't think I'm the kind of person that you know. If something happens to me, I get sick
16 or whatever then I'm gonna say, oh, you're gonna give me more pills, you're gonna do this. That
17 you know I can't die now. I mean, I wouldn't do that. I don't believe that you should be kicking and
18 screaming to try to live another day or two. You know we're gonna die. I've got a lot to die.
19 Anyway, I know that you should know that Everybody dies. We're here on a temporary deal, just
20 like the planet we live on. It's not forever. It's for a long time, but it's not forever. We're not forever
21 either. And, when you consider who we belong to and who put us together and who created that,
22 it's not that he's creating people every day and hair, eyes and nose and whatever. No, he created
23 a system to do this , just a replicating system. It's beyond anything that the human mind could ever
24 think of, mind could ever think of, never could think of, or, you know, create that.
25
26 I was also listening to somebody as well, I think it was on a YouTube channel, sometimes a
27 religious channel speaker, and he was going on about the elect that. It's some place. I can't
28 remember the name, the verse or whatever it was, but it's in the Bible. So we're God and, I
29 suppose, the word Jesus. We're discussing the fact that the elite would be the ones that would be
30 saved and they knew in advance exactly who they are or who they would be. Now if that's the
31 case. What percentage of human beings are elite? Are they elect? And how would you know? And
32 the fact that God knows, knew in advance and planned for this, planned that Jesus Christ would
33 have to die for this elite or elect to make it through this world in one piece and be acceptable to

him in the next world, that's quite a plan. That's greater than any plan that human nature or men or women could ever devise..

There's things that people say, oh, that can't be. I tell you it can be, the things that God has in mind for us. We haven't even thought about it, we can't even imagine it, not alone should wake people up. Should wake a person up and say, oh boy, there's a lot to look forward to here, and there really is a lot to look forward to for human beings that believe what God says, not what the professor says or a politician says or a preacher says. I shouldn't say everything a preacher says is wrong.

Some people are most likely pretty good that they don't tangle up on their own tangent and forget what God has said about things. There ought to be a lot of that. When you have thousands of different kinds of churches and there's only one correct way to believe it, you know there's problems, but anyway, that shows how valuable you are when you consider just your eyes alone. All valuable, priceless. God looks at you being priceless. That's hard for a person to swallow, isn't it? And thank goodness it's that way, though. So, being you're priceless, I'm glad I met you. I haven't met you yet, but maybe I will someday. In the meantime, I'm going to ask God to bless this priceless person you are, and we'll see you later.

Navigating the Erosion of Self: A Reflection on Individualism, Faith, and the Age of Global Uncertainty

Chapter17

Have you ever felt like just another face in the crowd, especially in the whirlwind of 2020? Our latest episode takes a deep dive into the concept of individualism, or rather, its unsettling decline amidst global upheaval. We'll examine a prediction from nearly a century ago that now echoes with chilling relevance, as masks become ubiquitous, symbolizing safety but also a loss of personal identity. Beyond the fabric covering our faces, we grapple with the profound implications of fear as a totalitarian tool and the prophetic visions of a society transformed. The conversation doesn't stop there; we also delve into the power of faith in these unprecedented times, highlighting the Bible's enduring promise of salvation through belief.

As we navigate the complexities of the world around us, we can't help but marvel at the grandeur of creation, from the cosmic expanse to the miraculous self-healing human body. Our discussion spans the seismic cultural shift from rugged North American individualism to the interconnected global village of today, raising critical questions about the fabric of our society. Amidst these reflections, we also share personal anecdotes on how technology, like a simple interaction with Alexa, offers unexpected companionship in solitude. Whether it's questioning the efficacy of pandemic measures or the companionship of artificial intelligence, this episode promises to stir your thoughts and challenge your perspectives on individuality, faith, and our collective future.

Good morning. October 29, 2020, 803 am Not a bad day. It's kind of warmed up a little bit. We have pretty cold weather, a lot of rain or snow. I was warming up. I think November, you know, also has to be better than October. The reason why, you know, sometimes a person gets an idea or something and it bugs them. And what bugging me today is Something I had not really realized, you know, and I read something about a guy who wrote Something I didn't know in his book 90 years ago, mentioned his name and everything else, and he what? What he was writing about is the loss of individualism and he said people will, worldwide, would end up wearing masks at one time, which would allow them to be stripped of their individualism and would allow Totalitarian regimes to take over and you know, It wouldn't be a democracy of any kind anymore and it would be brought in by fear. Well, I thought what, more of a description of 2020 is that the idea of Loss of individualism is Is big. I mean, it's a big game changer.

People are so Manipulated, can be so manipulated by fear, that it's just amazing. I mean, if somebody told me that before I said come on, no, that's just, it doesn't have to be fear. That is, you know, shaking in your boots, fear of anything. It can be just a low-level fear, or something looking back over your shoulder, whatever that drives people to do these things. And it seems like, if you don't conform, that's the big fear.

And that's exactly what's happening and you know people are at least somebody like me, who don't really realize what takes place to bring about all these big changes. God has predicted them..
Most likely most people don't know how it's gonna happen, but there it is and right in front of you,

1 and it's happening right in front of you. And the loss of individualism. That's what's happening now,
2 right now.
3
4 And the thing is, it's not local, it's worldwide. So it's oh Well, I believe that God calls you by name.
5 God knows your name. Satan will call you by a number. But to take over the world, to control the
6 whole population of the world, has to be a pretty, pretty dastardly devious system. But I think that's
7 exactly what's taking place Right in front of our eyes. It may not happen right at all at once. Maybe
8 we may get over this but it will have been already proven that it can be done and all it takes is
9 some good reason and people will fall in line immediately. You know what really Worries me is that
10 you know, I believe what God says and I believe what the Bible says.
11
12 I don't necessarily believe what man made religion say, because I don't believe that. I don't think
13 they have the power to Do that. There Hundreds and hundreds of different religions and all
14 claiming to be right. That's wrong, it's not true. But the Bible itself and the words of Jesus have to
15 be true, otherwise there's nothing. So it's always amazed me that you know, no matter how much
16 you want to rail against something, you can't change it. So the only other thing to do is realize that
17 this is all a plan and for sure that Jesus came to do what he did To save the people who believe.
18
19 And the funny part about it is how this can be based on belief. That's it. You can't work for it. You
20 can't do anything. And that to me, that is such a strange thing. But that's the way God works, and
21 he knows everybody's thoughts. He's created us. He knows every single cell in our body and when
22 we are created works, we are given a spirit. God gives every single human being a spirit, the
23 minute that can see, and when they die, the spirit goes back to God again and waits there till it's
24 called. So the thing is that you know, in God's view it's totally, absolutely important what you
25 believe, the things you do as a result of your beliefs, that's different.
26
27 But to do something to get to so that God has to give it to you, that doesn't work. Now, he and this
28 business of God, knowing who he's going to, going to have in his kingdom, who he isn't I'm not too
29 sure about that, but it does. A lot of places it looks like that's the case. That's been predetermined.
30 But maybe it's. Maybe it's predetermined up to a point and then it's left to see. Because he leaves.
31 He leaves human nature with choice. They have a choice.
32
33 The only time we know that is available to human beings to have a choice. They can choose
34 Because he has a real son.

He has a son that chooses him as his father and wants to .When I see the Direction, things are going. It's going fast. I mean all these things that are Basically anti Christ, anti God, then get me. They've taken God out of them, worshiping in a lot of places that are trying to get rid of, trying to get rid of religion altogether, taking it out of schools, taking it out of Business, whatever, not allowed to some places You're not even allowed to Preach it. Soon there will be a lot. They soon will come along and call it hate speech, which they've already said, because Now you have all kinds of Things that are that God is definitely against, and people who are half way reasonable, note Now they can say oh, they don't, I don't believe a Bible, I don't.

Who could write them? A lot of them. That's not right. It's the only communication that the Creator has given to his creation and Instead the test of time. I mean so what I said a couple thousand or two thousand years now or more, but it was written over 1500, You know the Idea, basically what I see is so, so big. You know, just absolutely vivid is the Direction that people are taking, where they reject God. They just reject God.

They have no fear of God's judgment. That's a big problem and this generation, and maybe the generation just before this Maybe it's the last, I kind of think it's his last generation, which is usually 33 to 40 years old. The ones who have rejected basically, in a nutshell, have rejected thought. I'm wearing these Dark sunglasses today because I was in the hospital yesterday and both of my eyes operated on him. They're pretty puffy and red and I was bleeding, but then the quick bleeding now,. I don't know if I'm gonna get blocked eyes or what, but I told the surgeon there, who's a nice guy. I saw him, I said I was laying there and I said okay. I said I want you to give me an ironclad guarantee that these rolls that's what you're doing will last for another 86 years. He laughed and he said absolutely. Basically, he just did a thing to tighten up my bottom eyelids, which are sagging down, and he called it n and threw toppy or something like that, I don't know. Well, he said. I meant you know right, the right eye was the worst. And he said well, I'm gonna do both, but I stitch up this one and stitch up the other one. Pull them, put stitches in them, just pull them back up. I don't know if it's gonna work or not when we talk for about three quarters of an hour, maybe not even that. I was in and out of there, I froze both eyes, just froze them, couldn't fail. It's cutting away and stitching and pulling.

But anyway, this idea of a loss of individualism is a big flag. It shows that we're going into a situation in this world which is going to be a one-world government for sure, and we may get by

1 with it for maybe another few years. I think one of the big things will be how the election goes in
2 the United States in a couple of days. If it goes to Trump, it most likely will be held up for another
3 four years anyway. But after that the socialists, communist people are whatever are going to get in
4 and individualism and democracy is what people call it, which is one. True, anyway, but it's, it's
5 only it's the one that's been running the western world for the last 200 some years or more, but it's,
6 you know, it's not perfect and, and what the thing is, that's got nothing to do with it.
7
8 God's timetable is the one that has. That's the thing. His timetable is coming, it's going to be done.
9 It doesn't say that on December the 24th this is going to happen. It says this is going to happen,
10 watch for. It doesn't say when, because time is not something that God actually deals with us. He
11 deals with it differently because he's outside of time, but everything he said will be done and
12 there's no doubt about it. He knows the exact minute. It's going to be done, but he doesn't tell us. if
13 I asked you how many, whatever, what? How many people do you have? How many people are in
14 your army? If you say we have many people in the army, what is many? What do you mean by
15 many thousand, two thousand?0ne Million.
16
17 The thing that I, from what I understand, is when God says many, God does not embellish
18 anything. He never exaggerates like we do. He just says I will have many sons. Christ is the
19 firstborn of many sons. What is that? Could be millions, billions, because things done on God scale
20 are so horrendously big and large that it's way beyond what we can imagine.
21
22 When I think of just the creation, I mean that's a big thing. You look at creation. You see the sun,
23 moon, star, earth, rivers, mountains, nature. You see all that, but then you don't look at the
24 mechanics of it. It gets smaller and smaller and smaller and more precise and more you know. You
25 get down to atoms and neutrons and whatever. And they still have systems and you can't see
26 them. They're so small but they all have systems. And when you look at that you say how often?
27 What is this? Lots of mystery.
28
29 If and keeping on. The only thing you notice is all the wrinkle ranch. I'm living at wrinkle ranch,
30 where there are a lot of old people now. The thing is, what happens is I don't get wrinkles. What
31 happened is I got too much skin. The skeleton shrinks and the skin doesn't. So that's just a.fact.
32 They should just pull it all up here, cut it off, put, tighten the whole thing up, cut it off and not get rid
33 of the excess skin. And you look around at people. They're all got flab skin hacking here here,
34 jowls underarms oh god, they could do night skin too all over the place.

1
2 But anyway, the main thrust of what I'm talking about today is individualism, and it's so. I could just
3 feel it. When I heard this I just thought this guy is right on. How come he wrote this 90 years ago
4 and just now people are realizing not that he's a great person or anything. He was just an ordinary
5 guy who had some kind of vision of this or whatever. And it just shows that God has his own time
6 for doing things. And it's like I was planning. I booked a few out of 11 days at the port of Viarta and
7 then back to San Diego and then a 70 cruise down to Mexico and back again on the Koning
8 Coronavirus, whatever you wanna call it is one micron, so it could easily just come in anyway.new
9 ship. Sounds like a pretty good little holiday actually, but I don't know if I'm going to go the way it
10 sounds. I may not because people are fearful.
11 I'm pretty sure that the end result would be pretty close to the same. Wearing a mask doesn't stop
12 that. I mean. It's scientifically not even possible. A mask will filter out. I think things down to what
13 they call three micrometers. It's very small, but they claim, like the coronavirus, china virus,
14
15 . But that's most likely very, very true. One moral government is what's on the table, and that's
16 been thwarted quite a few times. But it's there and it's coming one way or the other, and I can see
17 the way
18 way it's gonna come. I didn't realize this before, but I can see now.
19 \Now there's less agriculture, less farming area, which means less individualism. Farming was
20 individualism.
21
22 I grew up on a farm, a little economic unit. Ours was 320 acres, most of them were 160 acres.
23 There was no government money of any kind or support or anything. Didn't even think about it.
24 You looked, everything had to come from the land of that farm. It had to be grown. It was
25 agriculture. I don't care if it was timber, grain, beef, hogs, chickens, cats, milk, whatever. It all came
26 off the farm and we lived on the farm. That's what it was. It was an actual economic unit. It was like
27 a little farm factory.
28
29 According to Wikipedia, a farm is an area of land that is devoted primarily to agricultural
30 processes, with the primary objective of producing food and other crops. It is the basic facility in
31 food production. The name is used for specialized units such as arable farms, vegetable farms,
32 fruit farms, dairy cake and poultry farms, and land used for the production of natural fibers, myofuel
33 and other commodities.
34

1

2 You're welcomeDo you hear that? Yes, that's the way I have now. Believe this or not? I have two

3 dots on Alexa Echo and two Alexa 8-inch shows.

4 .

5

6 Alexa. Stop, I live alone with Alexa so she's my only company. That's something. Do you live with

7 a false voice and burst? That fits the times. The thing is that All this was going on. Now just turn

8 the TV on. If you watch TV Like I do, you know I usually would watch the news, whatever, but most

9 of my watching now is on YouTube and I'll go to I'll go to both sections or go to I'll go to some other

10 deals I'll go to. I'll pick up Some people that I really like listening to, and one of them is an

11 Englishman named Derek Prince.

12

13 He's dead now but he Preached for many, many, many years. He's a stiff old Englishman and he

14 was in the British Army and he was also in the universities and England. You know thanks, you

15 know Oxford and all that and he allows, all of a sudden, he is what he is in the army. When he got

16 converted, I guess it was a real conversion, because he ended up on the floor and Laughing and

17 crying, doing all kinds of things on the people in the cat and the barracks didn't know what to do,

18 took until morning to get over it and he was changed. He said he had changed completely. He

19 used to be a pretty rough guy I guess, but whether he's very nice or not nice, he's a very precise

20 person to listen to.

21

22 Everything he does is very precise. He speaks on a subject, he doesn't wander off. You know,

23 trying to be an entertainer I'm most preacher of. You are to entertain and put on a show. Without a

24 big show, who gets the biggest crowd? No, that's why I like listening to him. And there's another

25 Englishman, David possum. He's a. He's not pretty good, he's very good. He's English too, but I

26 think they're both dead now and, compared to the creatures that you hear these days, subtle, just

27 nuts, I mean nuts, I can't go for that stuff at all. can eat, they can do things, or what happens?

28 Spiritual food or something. And of course we can't. We can't fathom, we can only. Leave what it's

29 what he said and leave it up to. I mean, you can use your imagination, I guess, but yeah, I've got

30 to say something. It's like the way up the. I say those people will get pissed off with me, but I'm

31 gonna say it, and there's nothing I can do about it.

32

33 I thought it's the drift away from God's plan of things. For instance, it is very plain and it says in the

34 Bible a couple different places the hierarchy of God's plan kingdom is God the Father, then it goes

to Jesus Christ the son, then it goes to the man under Jesus and then the woman under the man. That's the hierarchy. That's not the way it's working, that's just and that's a rebellion against that.

Women are rebelling.

And why is it women? Why Is it? Because women are more susceptible to being manipulated that way. You know, I know it was I was gonna mention again, remind people. But the last thing Jesus said before he left this earth was do not be deceived. Watch that you are not deceived. There's deception going on like you wouldn't believe, and it appears to me that women are more susceptible to deception than men.

Up yet men Are getting very few of them anymore. I Mean I see, other than older people like me, younger people are Getting less and less male. They are getting effeminate Men, entertainers or something they sing like girls. They're either. They are either Feminine or there are some. You know a good percentage. I guess I'm not gay. That's all basically against God's will. God hates that and what's? That's what's happening and, mind you, that's exactly what he said was good. It's nothing that nothing happening that God didn't say. It's not a thing happening that God didn't say. What's going to happen, everything's coming up. The next thing on our table for us is when certain things are done. It has to be done in Israel, there has to be something happening with temples and Jewish people and whatever. I can't really say what it is all now, but that has to happen first.

And then the great deception place and the Antichrist comes up and rules the world for a few years, destroys basically just about everything, and then, Christ comes and destroys the Antichrist and takes over the world and runs it for a thousand years and then during that thousand years he puts everything down that's wrong on the earth, I guess, and at the very end he has another war and all the people who still reject God are destroyed. Then the earth is totally renewed. The earth is burnt to crisp all in fire. Heavens on the earth are both on fire.

never changes. That's the problem, not the problem. That's the thing. God does not change. People think they can say, oh well, we don't want to do that, we want to be this You know, and you know you want to live the way you want to live. Go ahead, it doesn't matter. Of course it matters. If you say it doesn't matter, why do you say it doesn't matter? If it matters? Deception, man or man? Jesus said don't be deceived. And how easy that is and how many are going to be deceived. Most likely millions, millions. That's the sad part.

1
2 There's so many people that could, and it's a thing that God has offered it as a free gift. You can't
3 buy it. You can't earn it. If you agree and you want and your desire is to be His Son, women will be
4 sons. If they go to heaven, they're not going to go to heaven. Nobody's going to go to heaven.
5 Heaven is coming to earth. That's plain and simple. There's like a religious talk of people going to
6 heaven and floating away to heaven and just bonkers. What amazes me is why God would pick
7 the earth on all planets in the universe. I've heard that the earth is situated in such a possession
8 that it can view out over the whole of the universe. It has a special position in the universe. Now,
9 whether the universe is going to disappear or not, God says that it will be a new heaven and a new
10 earth.
11 is just heavens, that means stars or whatever. So when we hear about the big black hole leading
12 up the Milky Way, who knows? Maybe that God is putting them in the whole universe in black hole
13 canisters. For maybe later sometime, I don't know. Anyway, I better quit right now. That's enough
14 for today. Thank you very much If you listen. Thank you
15

Life So Far - Exploring Tattoo Culture, Body Modifications, and the Role of Faith

Chapter 18

Do you ever stop to ponder the profound transformations society has undergone over the past four decades? Today, we journey through time reflecting on how the planet has shifted, particularly highlighting the boom of tattoo culture and body modifications. We urge you to join us as we dissect the motivations behind these decisions, considering the roles of vanity, defiance, and the sway of pop culture. We challenge the dominant narrative, emphasizing that our bodies are divine creations and not simply canvases for our whims.

Delving deeper, we also contemplate the weighty consequences of straying from God's laws and the incomprehensible vastness of His promises. We discuss how hope and faith play a pivotal role during challenging times, instilling in us the strength to weather the storm, even when we don't

1 know when it will pass. The assurance is that God does, and we can trust in Him. So, come and
2 explore with us as we offer a fresh perspective on how we view our bodies and the role faith plays
3 in our lives.
4
5
6 I'll give you the temperature in Vernon, BC, right now it's just a pretty nice 79. That's not bad.
7 That's Fahrenheit. I think I told you I like Fahrenheit because it's warmer. I'm trying to set the lights
8 here right. Anyway, we're coming to the end of July. All over the world it is the end of July, which
9 means summer is just about three quarters done. Pretty close, that's how fast that happens, and
10 that happens in North America, Australia's middle of winter exposed.
11
12 Anyway, what I want to talk to you about today is something that bothered me for a while, but it's
13 also one of these things. I don't know what I can do about it, except I can see the repercussions of
14 this is somebody's gonna pay and that is people who don't understand and maybe don't want to
15 understand God's sayings and God's laws and rules and proclamations, whatever the things that
16 he says are good and not good. Don't do this, you'll do that now. When I grew up I kept harping
17 about this, let's say, let's go back in time, say 40, 40 years, that would be 1967, number 60, 70s in
18 the 70s or something. The hippie movement started in 1960 but I, growing up with young guys all
19 over the place, some people doing all kinds of stuff, I never saw one guy with a tattoo, not one that
20 I saw, and I knew that you weren't supposed to have tattoos. I knew that from going to church. I
21 guess I went to church and some eight years old, nine years old, and I guess maybe it was a little
22 bit in the catechism and stuff like that, I don't know. But it appears now that in these last, like all
23 this stuff I'm talking about, you know, great abortion, drive.
24
25 Now tattooing really didn't get started in Canada, here anyway, or the United States. I don't think it
26 was too much difference, you know, until maybe I don't know maybe in the late 90s, 2000, 90s or
27 something like that. You see, I used to see the tattoo parlors popping up, you know, but that was
28 like in 2000 and something. And I'd say to people well, when you get the tattoo parlors downtown
29 where other businesses can't make it, you know there's a problem. Now there's tattoo parlors all
30 over the place, not a whole bunch, but there's quite a few. Never was before.
31
32 Now, why is that? Is that rebellion doing that? Or is it vanity or what it seems like? All you have to
33 do is have a famous person get something and the rest fall. And all these especially the men, I
34 should say that's not just men. Tons of women are tattooed now and that, I think, is really bad,

1 because they're ugly.
2
3 I mean, there's nothing nice about tattoos that I can see, disfiguring a perfect body that God has
4 given them. That's the absolute fact. They didn't create their body. They didn't get it at Walmart or
5 downtown at the store anywhere. No, sir, God had a plan to create bodies for each person alive.
6 And when they say it's my body and I can do what I want, that is absolutely not true. I didn't get
7 this body, I didn't buy it. I woke up in it and it's God's body that I'm living in. He provided me one to
8 travel in, to live in, to do whatever.
9
10 It's only going to last for a certain period of time. It deteriorates. It's like everything else in this
11 world Everything deteriorates, everything wears out, dies, disappears, regenerates, dies,
12 disappears Everything. But why is it? I don't know any better. Is that the problem? Like I watch
13 even black skinned people tattooing. They really have to tattoo and they have to get black, blacker
14 than they're black, and then browns in between and different colors in between, and they have to
15 do one solid arm. They don't really want to do it on the other, but they want to do one. And then of
16 course, there's the nose pins and the rings and the ear rings and the. Now God says don't do that,
17 don't do cuttings, do
18 I remember going into Walmart and I came up and I saw this girl at the teller. She was basically a
19 very attractive girl, except she was totally defaced. Yeah, if you had taken off all those rings and
20 stuff and tattoos and what else, she would have been a very beautiful girl, but with that on she
21 looked like that, she looked like the devil, terrible. And women I hate to say this, but they're terrible
22 copycats and they will copy everything that comes along. And when I see the odd young, you
23 know, 19, 18, 20-year-old who has no tattoos and who has, you know, real nice skin, you can say
24 what you like, but white skin women are very attractive, more attractive usually than the dark skin
25 Not all. There's dark skin beauties too, but it's really sad because they're doing it at the detriment.
26 **Arlo Johnson:** 9:04
27 Now what I wonder is God says don't do this. Your body is not yours. I bought it with a price. I paid
28 for your body and if you know, that body is most likely not the body that is going to be resurrected,
29 but maybe that's a good thing. But for people to actually do that, that kind of means that they're
30 rebelling against their Creator. And to me it is a sign of you know the debauchery and the thing
31 that the world is just grinding down to the lowest, meanest, dirtiest common denominator you can
32 get. And I think we're quite a ways from the bottom yet, because I'm quite sure that God is going to
33 let this go on until it can't get any worse, until it's totally depraved. Then he'll say well, there you
34 are. That's what you've done, against my laws, against everything I said. Now, there's no way.**Arlo**

But this business of people not asking for forgiveness, doing stuff that God absolutely says no to and does not want people to do, does not want his sons to do, sons who are supposed to learn or be able to live with him in eternity, forever, and the people that ignore that, I'm sure that it's getting to be more and more and more, and there it is more. There are less and less and less and less people who actually care about what God says. I'm positive about that. I'm positive that it's getting less. I mean they can say all they like about it, the revival things or whatever there may be, but it will be God that will create, cause it. It won't be like I man, I couldn't save anybody, that's all, and I don't think you could either. You can be.

God said be a witness. Jesus said well and be a witness for me. That's all he said. He didn't say I, save people in my name. And I mean they. You know it's a lot of them, like you know. Oh well, I went to a camp meeting, I went to this and I'm saved. You know, I don't know about that, it could be whistling dixie too, but I mean they might be well on their way to doing something like that if they're really humble and honest about it.

God knows exactly, exactly if you're honest about it, if you mean what you say. That's why being humble means it's so important to him. You know, he debases the proud and he uplifts and raises the humble. What would you rather be, proud and debased, or humble and raised up? Pretty simple to this and a lot of the problem with all the stuff that's going on. You know I hate to say it and I hate to think about it, but it's going to get worse, even if, even at my age, I'll hate to see it. But it was going to happen Because people, people are worse than sheep, they are absolutely terrible.

You know the few that do listen and believe what God has said, and a lot less than there are those who say forget it, I'm not going to do that, oh, this is just a joke, this is just made up stories. It's not made up stories. You can't say that the world is a made up story. You can't say nature is a made up story. You can't say your eyeball is a made up story. Let's see you create an eyeball and make vision, for instance, for millions and billions of people, put in a system that just works and multiplies itself, just totally automated, an automated system that populates this world with people, humans and you know that's a miraculous thing right there.

Arlo Johnson: 16:37

And I think that the thing is, if anybody had a glimpse, a bit of Common sense, even they would know that God has rules for people. They're not rules for him there, rules for all the people that

1 might live with him, and if they break all those rules, they're breaking God's laws. God's laws are
2 absolutely Made in stone. Whatever they don't change and God says I don't change you, never
3 changes you and me. It's like they can change and do this change and do that fashion this way, do
4 that. Now they think they can lie and get away with it continually. Well, they can do it, but they
5 won't get away with one Iota. God controls time. He has all the time of work. As he controls time,
6 he's outside of time. He created time, and Time will be no more. It'll stop. There won't be any more
7 time, earthly time.

9 But what are you spotting? What is the person supposed to do? Except, I Don't ask God to Draw
10 these people away from that, or for their own good or something. I guess you can do that, but
11 other than that, I don't really know what you can do. The only thing is to avoid it. I've avoided it at
12 all costs and if you have a good friend that's doing that, you should let them know. You Know
13 Some of these women who have these tattoos.

15 What are they going to look like when they're 60, 70 years old, 80 years old? Can you think I'm
16 gonna imagine that I Don't see any in the people that I see that are older, right here where I live,
17 they didn't ever have that. But the people coming up there's all kinds, who will be 80 someday, 70,
18 80. What are they gonna look like? Well, the only good thing is there is an end to all this. There's
19 an end. Whether we like it or not, God has declared an end to this stuff. He'll decide when and
20 where and how and everything, but I mean he's told us Totally what's gonna happen Should not be
21 a surprise to anyone. And after that comes the Judgment..

23 The thing to do is to think about this way if you make it through this world and are able to Get over,
24 overcome a bunch of things that are wrong, that you do and people have end up doing, and
25 Overcome them, and God says you will actually you will be with him if you overcome these things.
26 And Then the promise is so great I Mean, if we can't even Even talk to you or whatever else how
27 great it is because we can't explain it. We don't have words to explain that. All we can say is what
28 the promises are. And the thing is it is so different night and day from this life, totally different. God
29 says if you lose your life, you gain it. If you lose your life from my sake, my laws and my gospel,
30 you gain it. If you don't, you could lose it. Those are the things that are different. That's not man-
31 made ways at all, that's God-breed ways, totally different than man does. I still say it's if we live in
32 a world it would be a lot simpler and a lot better if we went by God's time and God's calendar and
33 all that. Why we didn't do that, I don't know. It's because we think we know better. That's the
34 problem.

1

2 So, with July just winding down and I heard this morning they didn't call it good global warming or
3 anything, but they said they had 450 forest fires in British Columbia this morning 450. And in
4 Halifax, Nova Scotia, which is east, on the other side of Canada, I think it's three or four miles
5 away north of New York and whatever is on the coast, they got two feet of rain in one day. Two
6 feet, I feel. A lot of water, boom, flooded like crazy. I am amazed by the water. I may book the
7 cruise again, That's where God's kingdom is going to be. Can you imagine that heaven is going to
8 be where we are? We don't go to heaven. It comes here While we go off here for a while, I guess,
9 while the earth is being purged and cleansed and whatever else. Then His city comes down, a city
10 that's bigger than most countries, bigger than France, bigger than Texas, bigger than British
11 Columbia and most of Alberta, 1500 miles square. You just like, right here in Vernon, bc, you have
12 to go right to Los Angeles to do one side. That means going out of BC, Washington, Oregon,
13 California and then I have to go the other direction. How many states would that be? So that's
14 going to cover a huge portion of this planet. I don't know how this is going to work because it's
15 1500 miles high. I mean, it's just going to. I don't know. Let's imagine that's all being looked after
16 and you've got an attorney to look around and figure that out, or look at it, study it, do something
17 about it.
18

19 I'm sure that nobody is going to be just standing and sitting around. There's going to be things to
20 do. Because you have the power to do so many things and then your spiritual perfect body. I better
21 quit. But I don't know. I hope you have something to hope for, because without hope there is not
22 much you can do.
23

24 You have to have hope. You have to have a reason to get up in the morning and to live. Even if
25 bad things are happening all around and people are doing whatever. You have to say well, there is
26 a better day coming. Most likely, there are going to be some rough ones in between. You know
27 you can make it, we can make it,
28 I guess, and if we don't, we just go to sleep with our fathers and wait.
29

30 We are not in control of that. Don't know about that. Only God knows about that. Jesus told
31 pepole that information personal to Him. Nobody else knows when. So until then, I hope you have
32 a good evening and a good day. God bless you, and I mean that. I'll thank you in advance for it. So
33 God bless and goodbye.
34

Manufactured by Amazon.ca
Acheson, AB

13520419R00057